WHY WE FARM

WHY WE FARM

FARMERS' STORIES OF GROWING OUR FOOD
AND SUSTAINING THEIR BUSINESS

BY ELVIRA DIBRIGIT

Cover and Interior Design by Ashley Halsey
Photos provided by the author, Todd Gettleman
or the farmers themselves, unless otherwise noted.
Editors: Aaron Sikes and Meredith Tennant

ISBN: 978-0-692-84063-4
10 9 8 7 6 5 4 3 2 1
First Edition

Published by Rumsey Press
PO Box 24
Rumsey, CA 95679

RUMSEY PRESS

Books may be purchased in quantity and/or special sales by contacting the publisher or the author at: info@WhyWeFarmCapay.com

TABLE OF CONTENTS

FOREWARD

Why *We Farm* weaves together the stories of some of California's most unique and visionary farmers. Nestled in the Capay Valley, these humble pioneers' moral and social compasses are truly aligned towards land stewardship and building community.

Elvira DiBrigit aptly describes the Capay Valley as an 'agricultural gem' and her vignettes about its farmers are inspirational, beckoning a new generation of farmers to the land that sustains us. This little valley can be likened to many agricultural regions of the United States, it's history can be seen as a microcosm of agricultural development around the country. If we can take the lessons learned here into the future, we will be going in the right direction. Paul Muller from Full Belly Farm says it best, "You know, the Garden of Eden never disappeared. If you're humble enough, you can be part of its manifestation."

In each of her interviews Elvira shares with the reader the hope that every farmer has: to be successful in developing a long and rewarding relationship with the plants, the people and the land that all grow our food.

The interviews with over a dozen of the valley farmers remind me of my own beginning farmer experiences over forty years ago. As a first generation farmer I struggled with the culture of agriculture. By culture I mean, figuring out how to be successful on the land. With variable weather, fluctuating labor availability and market prices and the huge cost of land and water, the odds of a beginning farmer making it are slim. Elvira does not shy away from these business realities in her interviews, yet her book ultimately strikes a chord of hope by celebrating the wisdom and experience of those small business people who work the land.

—Craig McNamara

Owner of Sierra Orchards
President of California State Board of Food and Agriculture

INTRODUCTION

When I first moved to the country, farming for a living seemed magical to me; just plant a seed and it will grow. But as I got to know my neighboring farmers over the last twenty years, I realized that much of their work involves problem solving. The history of agriculture is just one act of human ingenuity after another, and this continues into the present day. Many of the farmers I interviewed for this book are experimenting constantly. They are trying out various ways to deal with drought conditions, such as no-till methods and the use of different cover crops. They are following new research about soil microbes and integrated pest management. At the same time, they are navigating complex issues such as labor laws and water rights.

I was deeply impressed with the farmers I met, as people and professionals. I wanted to know more about the impulse that got these people started in farming, and the realities of their daily work. I saw them working long hours in any weather and then working overtime to drive their produce to market, not to mention raising children and participating in community organizations. I wondered, How did they manage it all? Were they really making a living? What circumstances helped them to succeed? These are the types of questions I asked in my interviews.

This book offers anecdotal stories about farmers from one valley, each practicing different agricultural methods: from conventional to organic, from wholesale to mail order, from single specialty crop to wide product diversity. There are stories of young farmers and old farmers, single-family farms and corporations. There are farmers with state of the art technology, and others using only hand tools and walking behind tillers. The profession of farming certainly has no one "right" way.

Capay Valley is a small agricultural gem, only one and a half hours from the San Francisco Bay Area. It sits nestled between the foothills that separate it from the Central Valley to the east and Napa Valley to the west. Cache Creek carries water down the valley floor, fed by Clear Lake and other tributaries. In the upper valley, one of the oldest privately run irrigation canals, the Rumsey Ditch, brings summer water to over five hundred acres. The high summer temperatures and light winter frosts make for long growing seasons. For many thousands of years, the valley has offered a rich bounty to the people who lived here. Descendants of the Wintun people are still farming here, as you can read about in the chapter on Seka Hills.

In many ways, Capay Valley can be seen as a microcosm of what's been happening on a national scale. There was a time when it was a booming agricultural area, with a train taking boxes of fruits, nuts, and vegetables to the cities. Then as the agribusiness model came to the fore in the 1950s, Capay Valley experienced a demise of small farms, a situation similar to many other areas in the United States. Property sat unused; orchards were left untended. There was a lot of fallow ground by the1970s. Nationally, there were 2.1 million farms in 2012, compared with 7 million in 1935, and the average farm size has gone from 290 acres to 434 acres. (Of course many farms are much bigger.)[1]

However, over the last thirty years we have seen a slow revival of rural life. And more recently there has been a surge of interest in farming. People are realizing the benefits of buying locally grown food. Chefs are featuring farm names on their menus. Bumper stickers are displayed that read, "Know your Farmer." Of the 2.1 million farms mentioned above, 88 percent were identified as small family farms with an average size of 231 acres. More people are wondering if farming could be a viable way to make a living.

There are various reasons that people have begun to work toward reinvent-

[1]. Farming and Food, edited by John Tarrant, New York, Oxford Univ. Press 1991 & USDA 2012 Census of Agriculture

ing agriculture. There are second- and third-generation farmers who have made changes in order to maintain the family farm. In the Capay Valley and nationwide, there was the back-to-the-land movement that has remained an undercurrent with each generation since the 1960s. The farmers I've met have sought to learn from the mistakes of previous generations, being practical in their lifestyle choices and strategic in how they market their products.

Farming often requires cooperation. The farmers in Capay Valley not only lend each other tools and share advice, they also practice "coopertition." Full Belly and Riverdog have been known to share space on one another's delivery trucks, even when they are competing for sales in the same markets. Skylark Ranch shares a farmers' market table with a neighboring pasture-raised livestock farm, Casa Rosa Farm. Together, the farmers are actively building community, exploring agritourism possibilities, and developing a brand for Capay Valley products.

There are a number of young farmers featured in this book, but the average age of farmers in America is 57 years of age and growing older. The number of farmers under 25 years old has decreased 20 percent in the last five years. All the farmers featured in this book know that they are part of the 3 percent: that's the percentage of the national workforce employed in agriculture. And they know that the task of future farmers will be to try and feed a planet of ten billion people. The United States is still the giant of the food world, dominating the world's export markets in cereals, soy, beef, and citrus. But there are real questions about how to meet growing demand, as soil and water resources are diminishing.

I've written this book out of my love for the land and the people of Capay Valley. People who stay in farming tend to be the kind of people who jump out of bed in the early morning, raring to go. Obviously someone only does this if they love their life. The people I interviewed were each grateful for the life they were living. By showing glimpses into the lives of these farmers and the diversity of farming methods in just one valley, I hope to inspire a new generation of farmers to take to the fields.

John Ceteras at the orange washer

BLUE HERON FARM

FARMING MODEL: ORGANIC, FAMILY OWNED

STARTED IN: 1975

OWNERS: JOHN AND GRETCHEN CETERAS

SIZE: 20 ACRES

MAIN CROPS: ORANGES, WALNUTS, AND GOURDS

In 1975, John and Gretchen Ceteras stood looking at an old, neglected almond orchard in Rumsey, California and knew immediately that it was the place they longed for. They moved onto the land, which is bordered by the creek and clay cliffs to the east, and the historical Rumsey Irrigation Ditch to the north. Since then they have transformed the farm with lush green orange groves, walnut orchards, and fields of vegetables.

John got started in agriculture as a kid in a small town backyard in Ohio, pulling weeds and caring for chickens with his father. "Garden grown is better than store bought" was one lesson John's father imparted to him. Gretchen's first years were spent on a farm in Oregon, but at an early age she moved to town, where her "farming" experience was limited to mowing the lawn and trimming the hedges. Still, like John, she knew her dream was to live close to the land.

Despite the Rumsey orchard being in a bad state and past its production peak, John and Gretchen attempted to keep the almonds going. Following the advice of their neighbors, they sprayed chemicals to ward off mites, fungus, and blights. "We

moved up here and did what the old timers told us to do," Gretchen says. "We didn't think about organic until after we had a child. Then we started asking ourselves if we really wanted to raise a child in this atmosphere of fear. Finally we took a leap and started using organic tools." The organic movement was just getting started at that time, and the valley attracted a cluster of newer farmers who began sharing ideas while experimenting in farming without synthetic chemicals. The green grass under the orchard trees might be a giveaway that Blue Heron is an organic farm, but the weeds here are kept in check and the fields look clean and well tended.

Gradually, John and Gretchen realized that the old almond trees would not support their dream of living off the land, so they began cutting down the trees that had the smallest yields and replacing them with Navel oranges. Eventually they took out all the old trees and replaced them with a few citrus varieties and a block of walnuts. The orchards are laid out squarely with plenty of room between trees for the tractor to mow. Blue Heron Farm is in the northern end of the Capay Valley known as the "banana belt." Because of the elevation and the close embrace of the hills, citrus does fairly well. But just in case a heavy freeze were to come along (as it has), the walnuts give the Ceteras another chance for having a crop to sell.

John and Gretchen have seen rough times; in 1977 there was a bad drought and then in 1983 there was a big flood. They have twenty acres on the deed, but one night during the flood they lost a couple of acres overnight—pasture, fencing, and oranges. As John puts it, "A big patch of clay just moved downstream." So now their A-frame house sits a little closer to the creek's flood plain, an open wilderness zone on the farm.

They are both equal owners of Blue Heron Farm. "We have a do-it-ourselves philosophy. We are not just farm managers, we are actually out there planting and picking." John and Gretchen cultivate and harvest Washington navel oranges, Valencia oranges, Clementine and Satsuma mandarins, Hartley and Chandler walnuts, Black Mission figs, and Early Girl and Sun Gold tomatoes, along with other tomato varieties. They have one full-time employee, and they hire one part-time helper for the orange harvest and two part-time helpers for the tomato harvest.

"Gretchen and I do the squash all by ourselves, picking in the early morning before the heat. We do the outside work in early morning and then move inside." Inside work for John means being on the phone, maintaining relationships with the produce buyers, while Gretchen does the bookkeeping. "Marketing takes effort," John says with a nod. "We are always thinking ahead and letting people know what we will be harvesting in a month, so we know who will be taking it and how we can get it to them at peak freshness. It's also important to let people know if we see a huge surplus coming up, or a shortage. You really have to start with marketing, so that you are certain there will be a place to sell what you grow."

Blue Heron was one of the first local farms to start selling to the Sacramento Natural Foods Co-op when it first opened in 1985. The handful of CCOF Capay farmers at that time would have monthly meetings, and one day "Sac Natch" came to that meeting looking for suppliers. John and Gretchen started selling them almonds and almond butter, then oranges, tomatoes, and squash. They continue to sell produce to Sacramento Natural Food Co-op to this day.

John knows that to make it in farming you have to invest continually, all the time, not just sporadically. "We have been in and out of debt, we borrow and pay back, borrow again. It all costs money: fertilizers, pest control, a new well and maintained pump; you have to be willing to make these investments because benign neglect will get you nowhere. We've seen people come along and plop plants in the ground, thinking that's all they have to do, but those people don't last long."

Over the years, they have had their share of pests to deal with. John used to be well known by his surrounding neighbors for the loud detonation sounds he would make with his Rodenator, blowing up gopher holes. This contraption injects and ignites a mix of oxygen and propane, creating a crushing pressure that kills tunneling rodents by concussive force. National organic standards have changed and the use of underground propane is not currently allowed. Consequently John has seen his gopher population increasing. Feral pigs have also become more numerous over the years. John tells me, "I shot a pig recently and it was so huge I couldn't move it! I didn't have time to take it to the butcher, so I just let the turkey buzzards make good use of it."

While farming is a busy, time-sensitive occupation, John and Gretchen have also done other jobs to bring income to the farm. John became the Rumsey Water Users Association superintendent shortly after moving to the area. This locally run organization dates back to the 1870's, when the Rumsey Ditch was created. The superintendent receives a small annual stipend for managing the head gates of the ditch, and keeping the water flowing from early summer to mid autumn.

Gretchen has been a substitute teacher with local districts for many years. They also have a nut-shelling machine and make a little money shelling walnuts for local organic growers. And then there are the gourds.

Gretchen's Dream Gourds artwork is a passion. She first grew gourds thirty-five years ago, with no idea what she would do with them. "I just loved the idea that something from the earth could preserve itself and be so useful as a storage vessel, water flask, musical instrument, or mask." She started wood burning and has gotten more artistic as her love for gourds grew. She has sold them at galleries and craft fairs, but soon found that it was more profitable to sell her art at the market, alongside their produce. They go to the Marin market, and even if she doesn't sell a gourd that day, at least she sells produce, and the booth cost is much lower than at a craft fair. The income from the gourds is only supplemental, but it fits into the yearly income well, selling more during holiday season, which is right in between tomato and orange seasons.

When asked about their biggest challenges, they immediately speak about water. 2015 was another big drought year and they were happy that they invested in putting in a new well a few years before, and felt lucky to have struck good water. Water quality in the valley varies a lot, even just a few yards away. "Our two neighbors dug wells and didn't do as well. We have another neighbor whose well water has heavy salts—they can't grow anything with that water."

Blue Heron Farm has the option to irrigate with water from the Rumsey Ditch during the dry summer months, but that water can become high in boron, which can be difficult for citrus to handle. So John doesn't like to rely on the ditch water toward the end of the summer.

It's on their mind that well water is finite; it comes from somewhere, and that source may run dry. Some wells are already going dry in the center of the valley. "This is worse than 1977. It's been a few years building up to this," warns John. "Sometimes we ask ourselves *What else would we do if we couldn't farm here?* Maybe we'd become cabinetmakers?"

But John and Gretchen are both clear that they want to stay in the Capay Valley. "We love living in a small community with a common thread, and the chance to be involved in a meaningful, direct way, such as the volunteer fire crew or the Rumsey Water Users Association." As John says, "In a small community, you either get off your ass and help, or your name is mud."

And they're both clear that they love farming, being surrounded by the sights of nature as they work. "We get to see the blue herons fishing along the creek, the hawks in the sky, and all the seasonal changes."

Charlie Opper (photo credit Todd Gettleman)

CACHE CREEK LAVENDER FARM

FARMING MODEL: SPECIALTY CROP AND VALUE-ADDED PRODUCTS

STARTED IN: 1996

OWNER: CHARLIE OPPER

SIZE: 1 ACRE

MAIN CROP: LAVENDER

Charles Opper makes a living off of one crop: lavender. He works fourteen-hour days, getting up before dawn and sometimes taking a siesta in the afternoon. "I don't have a weekly day off. Mondays are my slow day; I can't expect a lot out of myself after two market days and the long drive home. But by Tuesday morning I better hit the ground running or I'm falling behind fast."

Cache Creek Lavender Farm sits at the northern end of the valley, an open, flat, two-acre parcel. Along the western edge of the property runs the Rumsey Ditch, an irrigation canal built in the 1880s that brings water from Cache Creek. The rows of lavender lie out in the open sun. A modest farmhouse, covered with old white siding, is tucked behind a weeping willow and a rose garden. In the living room you're likely to find rows of fresh-cut soap on worktables. The intriguing smell of lavender pervades everything.

Charlie bought this property in 1994. He grows only an acre of lavender, which is a fairly low-maintenance crop. "Flower growing is great because you can do it so intensely," he emphasizes. "I found a niche and focused on it." Most of his time is spent making lavender products for the kitchen, home, and body, which he sells at weekend farmers' markets in the Bay Area.

He says he never really planned to be a farmer. He was working as an assistant manager of a golf course in Daly City when a friend asked him to take a look at an orchard they had just purchased in Guinda. "It was a beautiful place and I fell in love. I was given an offer to move up here as the farm manager. I was here only about six months when I accidentally set fire to Mike Perez's wheat field, so I got to know the neighbors quickly." Soon Charlie was working as farm manager for several places, helping city people who had bought orchards as second homes. He learned to do fertilizing, mowing, irrigating, helping with harvest and house repairs.

He feels fortunate to have found this community. "I spent a few years in Guinda, but when I began managing a place in Rumsey I really felt at home. The people up here are an interesting bunch and we bonded together during the renovation of the Rumsey Town Hall." When he was suddenly asked to leave his rental house, Charlie decided to look for a place of his own. He noticed an empty house in Rumsey, so he approached the owners to see if they were interested in selling.

"I really didn't have a plan when I bought this place. At that time, aromatherapy was a new 'in' thing with the general public; it seemed as though everyone was exploring the science of essential oils. My girlfriend, Linda, was studying plant and soil science and together we decided to try growing lavender, since we had this Mediterranean climate." One spring day, Charlie and Linda went down to Morningsun Herb Farm in Pleasant Valley and bought a couple thousand plants. "We had zero business plan. We were just having fun with no reason to think we had really hit on anything."

For a few years Charlie continued managing properties. Linda had a part-time job helping Jim Eldon of Fiddler's Green Farm sell at the farmers' markets. The first year that they had lavender to harvest was 1997. They sent a couple of buckets full of fresh lavender bundles to market with Linda on a Saturday. She came back that evening reporting that the lavender was gone in the first twenty minutes.

"The next week she went with six buckets full and sold out at $4 a bunch. The following week a dozen buckets were gone. By the end of the fresh cut season, which is maybe five weeks long, we were filling the truck up with buckets, maybe forty buckets with twelve to fifteen bunches each, and people were lining up to get their bunch of fresh cut lavender!" Charlie smiles and continues, "Like I said, no forethought went into this. We only had two back rows planted at that time."

After a couple of seasons selling the fresh cut lavender, Charlie and Linda were pretty sure they had stumbled onto something promising. Charlie decided to learn how to make soap. "I simply checked out soap-making books from the library," Charlie said with a shrug. He knew that there was more money in value-added products,

and also realized that they didn't have to grow all the lavender for the products they made. An acre of lavender can produce two to five gallons of oil, depending on the variety. Much like a winemaker will get grapes from different vineyards, Charlie buys some of his lavender from other suppliers. "I go through about fifteen gallons of essential oil a year. The soap I make is oil intensive, but that's what makes the soaps so nice. Factor in all the costs of the soap materials, including labels, and I'm only making like two dollars a bar. It doesn't sound worth the time, but it keeps customers happy and then other products we make have a better profit margin."

Charlie found suppliers in Sacramento for his soap-making ingredients, and Linda began making bath salts and drawer sachets. Soon they were taking trips to Europe to do research. "We spent a lot of time in Provence, France, where they grow English lavenders and produce really high quality essential oils. We'd come back with all kinds of ideas for new products."

Cache Creek Lavender has offered up to thirty-five different products over the time they've been in business. They have now weeded out the less popular things. "I have ideas for other products, but no time."

It was a slow transition to doing lavender full time. After growing the herb for a few years, Charlie and Linda started having their own table at the Menlo Park Farmers' Market as a seasonal vendor. Menlo Park had a farmers' market thirty years ago, before it was commonly popular, and it has many faithful customers. Some of these customers were editors at Sunset magazine, whose headquarters was in Menlo Park for many years.

As Charlie explains, "About twelve years ago, I was approached by Sunset magazine to do an interview. The writer had seen me at the market and thought we were interesting. The interview was for a short article highlighting several small farms that produce interesting crops and that were open to the public—I was told that from the beginning. But all I really cared about was that we were going to be featured in Sunset magazine. So I do the interview after market one day, and toward the end the woman asks me, *So when's your festival? When are you open to the public?*

"I had no answer really, because we had never been open to the public before. But I knew what she wanted to hear, so I said, *Well . . . we have open farm days when the lavender is in bloom, in June.* She was writing all this down, and as soon as she left I had to tell Linda, *Uh guess what, we are going to have an open farm day in June!*"

The first year it was just that, an open farm day, to tour the field and see where the products were made. But people read the paragraph in Sunset magazine and the phone started ringing, and they had a good turnout. Since then they've been doing it every year with a little more forethought. It's now turned into a two-day festival with music and food.

The story of Cache Creek Lavender Farm may sound enchanting, but Charlie is the first to admit that it can be stressful. "This year, planning the festival meant a lot of laying awake in the middle of the night, or just getting up at 3 a.m. to start my day. Linda is taking care of her elderly mother, so I'm doing it almost all by myself now." He started planning six months in advance, getting the music and food arranged, sending out press releases, and on top of that he has to keep making enough products.

Charlie's sister has been a big help since she retired and moved to the area. "She's amazing! She can watch a movie at night and make five hundred sachets. I'd be half crazy doing two hundred." He also hires help during the harvest season, and occasionally in the winter when the plants need pruning. He'd like to hire a book-keeper, but hasn't found a way to do that.

Making enough money to sustain the operation has been a challenge. Charlie says it's never been about the money. "It's been about what's the easiest way to make enough money to survive." But now he's looking for ways to generate more income. "I'm tired of scraping the edges to make a living." He is partnering with a wedding planner, to rent out his place for small weddings and elopements. "That's going to be a shot in the arm," he exclaims. And he is fixing up the house with the idea of offering farm stays, where people can come to experience life on a farm and sleep with the window opening onto fields of fresh smelling lavender. "The business model is changing," Charlie says confidently.

CAPAY ORGANIC

FARMING MODEL: ORGANIC FARM, FOOD DISTRIBUTION
    BUSINESS AND HOME DELIVERY

STARTED IN: 1976

OWNERS: BARSOTTI-BARNES FAMILIES

SIZE: 500 ACRES

MAIN CROPS: DIVERSE FRUITS AND VEGETABLES

There is a window view with daffodils popping up and peach trees loaded with pink blossoms when I meet with the three brothers of Capay Organic at the house where they grew up. The ranch-style house is now used just for meetings and family gatherings, but the brothers all have their individual memories of living here as boys.

"It was interesting because we all grew up at different stages of the farm," eldest brother Noah Barnes recounts. He and his twin brother, Che, grew up helping their parents do hand labor: picking tomatoes, bunching turnips, moving sprinklers. Kathleen Barsotti and Martin Barnes started the farm from scratch on twenty acres in 1976 with just a hand rototiller. "They were missing the mechanical ability; they didn't know how to even buy, much less how to fix equipment. So they were moving manure with a wheelbarrow because they could control that."

The middle brother, Thaddeus Barsotti, was much younger when their parents split up. In high school he learned how to drive a tractor from his mother's boy-friend, and early on he showed an aptitude for machinery work in the shop.

For youngest brother Freeman Barsotti, the farm was entering a different stage by the time he started helping. Kathleen started Farm Fresh to You, a door-to-door produce delivery business, in 1992. Freeman was put to work in the office, doing billing, making databases for customer service, or getting the delivery boxes ready for customers and making van runs to the Bay Area.

Freeman did get a little time out in the field. "We would always help Mom on transplanting days," he recalls. "I remember she would pull me and my friend Danny out of school in March to have us help transplant all day long."

What they all remember in common was growing up feeling financially strapped. They each shared memories of their mother getting stressed out that there might not be enough money to meet payroll. "This is what she talked about at the dinner table when we were children," Noah says.

"Ya," Freeman agrees. "I remember my mom saying *Why don't you boys ever say Gee Mom, thanks for paying the electrical bill. That's great that the lights turn on!* Toward the end of her life she had developed a life that felt middle class. I think that was important for her, and I know that rubbed off on me."

Thaddeus agrees that financial stability was something they all saw as really important when they sat down to discuss continuing the family business after their mother died of breast cancer in the summer of 2000.

"We were all doing our own thing," Noah shares. "Thad was finishing college, I had just started a job, and Freeman was in high school when Mom died. We all knew we were going to keep the business, so there wasn't really discussion of should we do it or not; we just came together and asked how?"

"We made some hard decisions," says Thad. "We hired Noah's fraternity brother to manage the farm for a bit while we got to the next stage of our lives." In just a few years the three brothers had all returned to work on the farm. Only Che opted

The Barnes-Barsotti families (Photo credit Megan Wilkinson)

to stay with his job as a pilot for the U.S. Coast Guard, though he continued to help with farm decisions and served on the board of Farm Fresh To You until his untimely death in 2009 during a search-and-rescue effort off the coast of San Diego.

I was wondering if the decision to come back to the farm had been difficult for any of them, when Thad starts to solemnly tell more of his story. "I thought I was going to be an engineer. I studied civil engineering with a focus on water. I was really good at it." He breaks into a smile, and I think this is going to be a bittersweet reminiscence of what might have been. "I had a job and when the boss would give me a week's worth of work, I would finish it in a day. I got so bored I would sleep under my desk." Then Thad breaks out laughing. "I realized then, *naw, I don't want to do this.* And I knew the farm was sitting here, so I came back and was motivated to make a go of it as a farmer. I haven't looked back since."

Their parents had done the hard work of starting a capital-intensive business from basically nothing. And what they lacked in mechanical knowhow, they made up for in customer service. "My parents were always better at marketing and understanding what the customer wants," says Freeman.

The home delivery business, Farm Fresh To You, started by Kathleen in 1992, got a big boost in 1994 after a *San Francisco Chronicle* article came out profiling the business. Kathleen was after the sustainable connection with the customer, year round. She started partnering with other farms to give the customers what they wanted, and from the start she always offered door-to-door delivery. The boys' grandparents lived across the street, and they used to do the deliveries out of the back of their old Buick. Soon after that article in the *Chronicle* came out, they were doing deliveries six days a week.

Another big boost was due to the serendipity of the business growing when the Internet was just developing. "Our mom had a veggie box customer, Bob, who called her up and asked to trade for a free weekly box if he made the farm a website. It was not the best website," Thad says with a grimace. "Just all kinds of colors spat out on the page. But it got our name out there."

On this early website, there was a rudimentary way that people could search for vegetables by name and find recipes. Kathleen had always provided recipes with the boxes and now, in the early '90s, she would get comments on her recipes from all around the world. "There was a period of a few years when we had no idea, but we had one of the best recipe websites in the world with thousands of people visiting our site. We could have been recipes.com, but we just thought it was random that people liked our recipes," laughs Freeman. "Our parents were so laser focused on what they were doing with the farm and door-to-door sales, they were blind to other opportunities. That's one of the differences now is that we are more strategic. We know that business is always going to be evolving; it's going to have to if we want to keep growing, so we try to keep track of other opportunities."

Freeman continues to explain. "Our philosophy is that we want to meet customers where they are and help them maintain that direct connection to farms. We always offer fruit in the box, and produce comes first from our farm whenever possible, then out to other local growers in concentric circles. Really, it's the service we are offering; we can get a lot of local product into people's lives by offering them this service with year-round selection of produce that people are interested in. If we offered only local in the box, there'd be no fruit around Feb. 15th. Citrus is ending then and cherries haven't started yet."

Produce box delivery services can have a lot of customer turnover as seasons change. Kathleen knew that if customers left the service for a time period, it wasn't that easy to just get them back when local fruit was available again a couple of months later. She left a legacy of being service oriented and working with other farms in other areas, in order to keep customers happy, and compete with retailers.

"There's a lot of talk about farm-to-table at stores and restaurants these days," says Freeman. "I can walk into a grocery market and see pictures of farmers hanging on the wall and signs about local food to make you feel warm and fuzzy. But when I look at the actual produce and where it's coming from, most of it is from Mexico or further. So that's the system we are competing with."

The brothers took their parents' legacy and expanded it. They recognize that they are lucky that there are three of them to divide tasks and work together to build something bigger. Thaddeus puts it this way: "We broke free from the inherent system in farming that good farmers work with wholesale middlemen who then work with the customers."

"What people may not realize about us," explains Freeman, "is that farming is a big part of what we do, but we are also running an entire food system." They have the farm, the home delivery business, the warehouse for packing boxes, and a sales and marketing team. They also opened the retail storefront, Farm Fresh To You, at the San Francisco Ferry Building.

The brothers see a trend in that more people want to work directly with the producers. They strive to maintain the connection between the farmer and the consumer, and they realize it doesn't have to be just their farm. "For it to work," says Noah, "we really have to get our hands dirty with other growers, asking *How can we work with you to help you with what you are doing?* You can't just be the middleman, taking for granted the farm, buying at prices that aren't sustainable. You have to understand what the farmers are dealing with. And I think we have the advantage in that we understand this more than any other middleman, having seen both sides of it."

Farm Fresh To You has a two-pronged strategy—working on customer outreach to educate the public and provide that customer service, then working with the growers to figure out what to grow affordably and with the quality that customers want. They work with small farms, offering help such as a food safety program, and sometimes partnering with them to grow a crop. They saw that there was a shortage of good organic growers and some of them who were growing a good product didn't always have a good economic plan. By buying from other farmers or partnering with them, they are increasing the grower base for organic agriculture. The Barsotti-Barnes brothers see that as a win-win.

"With farmers, there is not a question I won't answer," says Thaddeus. "Like *What's your plant spacing? How do you do projections? What's your budget? How do you pack the boxes?* We have fifteen years of figuring it out, and there are industry standards. I see other experienced farmers who want to hold that information close to their chest. But I'm like, *It's hard! I could show you the whole game plan and you'll probably still mess it up in the execution of it.* So about farming I'll answer any question people have. I think sharing information is important. And the reality is we are not the best at it; there are people who do it better than us."

One example of their innovation is the software they helped develop. When a customer signs up for a Farm Fresh To You subscription, they can go online to cus-

Photo credit Bill Goidell

tomize what they want in the box, and exclude items they don't want to receive. This gets even more impressive when the order gets to the West Sacramento warehouse where the box is packed. The software follows the box as it goes down the packing line. When the box gets in front of an item the customer wants, a light goes on and the employee packing that item knows to put it in the box. At the end of the line, the boxes are loaded onto a pallet according to their address and order of delivery. Developing this high-tech software really was necessary, considering that Farm Fresh To You now sends out thousands of boxes per month to homes.

The Barsotti-Barnes brothers want everyone to benefit from organic agriculture. Noah nods his head excitedly as he shares that he is moving up to Seattle soon with his family to start a new home delivery system in that region. "I'll be working with local growers up there and seeing what we can do. The innovation of the technology we've developed is big and we want to share it with the world. We feel this type of agriculture should be all over the world, and we know that we can't do that, as a farm. But we are interested in continuing to partner with others and share our model. We'd like to show others the way."

To this end, they also are excited about their "donate a box" program, which donated 10,000 boxes to food banks in 2015. The company obviously has a lot going on. United States Secretary of Agriculture Vilsack even took a tour of their facilities in September of 2011.

They have about 500 full-time employees, split almost evenly between the four teams of delivery, sales, warehouse, and farming. The company has gone through big transitions in the last ten years. Before that, the company was small enough that they all knew everything that was going on with the people and in the fields.

Sitting up in his chair, Thad says, "I distinctly remember the time I went out to look at a bare twenty-acre field, and I just stood there knowing we were going to plant this *whole* field into bunching greens—kale, collards—and feeling my palms sweat, it just felt *so big*. That same reality hits me looking at that number of 500 employees, too."

"Ya!" Freeman bursts out. "That makes my palms sweat when I think about it. It's like payroll is still haunting us," he laughs.

"But that's something we've really learned in the last five years," Noah says, nodding his head. "We've gotten better at knowing what type of person is good for which job. We have good managers."

"For me, personally," confides Freeman, "it's hard to beat a spring day on the farm; it's healthy for your soul." He gestures out the window at the blossoms swaying in the breeze. "But within the company, I really appreciate the beauty of working with a group to accomplish and make things happen. And believe me there are lots of hurdles! But I like working with a team and bouncing ideas back and forth. Looking back on our plan for the year and seeing that we did it and overcame challenges."

"There's a certain elegance," Noah continues, "in a farm where the farmer is handling everything, and they are the master of their domain, and they do it all. But the reality is, if that individual leaves then there is nothing. So we are building a company that can survive without us. It's all about having good people—that's all a good company is."

"Yep," agrees Thad. "There's a lot going on and it's fun! We are working together and making small changes in agriculture systems. I'm never bored here." He laughs. "We don't want anyone sleeping under the desk."

Tempranillo cluster

CAPAY VALLEY VINEYARDS

FARMING MODEL: FAMILY VINEYARD

STARTED IN: 1998

OWNERS: PAM WELCH AND TOM FREDERICK

SIZE: 25 ACRES UNDER PRODUCTION

MAIN CROP: WINE GRAPES

Sitting in the mission-style house on top of the hill, overlooking the grapevines, it's easy to assume that Tom Frederick and Pam Welch planned all this out from a blank canvas of raw land. Arriving by car, the manicured grapevines run perpendicular to the road, leading the eye up gentle, curving hills. There is a tasting room visible from the road, and tucked further down the driveway is an attractive new barn, housing the winemaking facility.

"The house was already here and we were just renting at first," says Pam, who is not related to the other Welch grape family. "People often ask, *Did you always want to make wine?* It really wasn't what we had in mind when we moved up here," she says. "We were looking for a place for Tom to set up his mechanic's shop, and we liked the view of the hills, so we settled here." Tom was in the business of restoring vintage race cars, after years of being a mechanic with racing teams. Neither of them

grew up with an agricultural background.

Tom and Pam moved up from San Francisco in 1979, but they didn't start planting grapes until 1998. It was another one of those old almond orchard stories. "Eventually we had to do something with this land of bumpy, rolling hills. Someone suggested we try grapes, but as far as we knew no one had ever grown them in this valley. So it seemed like a challenge."

The first thing they did, before they bought the property, was to have the water tested. Then later they had the soil tested. "The angst at the time was about nematodes, so we had that checked," recalls Pam. They had the soil ripped, to get the roots of the old almonds out. It took a year to get all the trees out.

One thing Pam and Tom learned quickly was not to take all the experts' advice on everything. They went to talk to the farm adviser at the County Extension office. His advice was to get a contract for the grapes before they even planted. "We came home and thought, *Who in their right mind would give us a contract? We've never grown grapes before and they aren't being grown nearby.* So we knew then that if we planted, we'd have to take it all the way to a marketable product, and that was the plan from that day on."

Pam and Tom took some weekend UC Davis Extension classes on viticulture, which they found very helpful. They read about trellising systems, and went to visit the people who sold the products, learning a lot from them. In the beginning they paid a professional vintner and a vineyard consultant to give them advice. "There were a lot of decisions to be made and everybody had their ideas of what was best, but we were the ones who had to choose."

Pam talks about how, when they started, the latest system for trellising was called the Smart Dyson. It is a system designed to increase grape production. With the cordon vine on permanent wire, the shoots are trained to go both up and down. "We went to see it at someone's vineyard, and when I saw it I immediately said, No Way! It was messy, with fruit on the ground and no way to walk down the rows. We had to go against the advice of almost everyone at the time because they all said it was the latest, greatest thing." Pam and Tom decided to put the cordon wire at forty-two inches, to make hand harvesting easier. As Tom puts it, "You have to be careful you don't fall for the latest theory just because. I mean, there are plenty of good ideas, if you can adapt them to all the ramifications of your own circumstances."

Capay Valley Vineyards started with six acres of Syrah and Viognier. They knew they would have to do things themselves or they'd be burning through a lot of money. "We did pretty much everything ourselves. Installing the trellising and miles of drip hose, and every single emitter we put in ourselves." Tom notes that infrastructure is at least 50 percent of the effort to begin with. And then sometimes there are things that need to be re-done. For instance, the first drip hose hangers they bought turned out not to be made of UV-resistant plastic. "That was one of the few failure items we had, but when you have 10,000 of them and they start failing on you. Oh, man!"

They have evolved systems over the years. The latest drip irrigation they installed is buried, rather than hanging on the wire. In addition to saving water, this makes it easier to walk and mow between rows, and prevents animals from nibbling on the hose.

"You don't want to have to go back and do things over again," Tom remarks. "So I try to be consistent and to anticipate the problems before they arise. Like with watering . . . you have to be on it before there is a problem. It's interesting to think about the farmers in days of yore, without all the technology we have today such as weather.com, or easy fencing and modern equipment. Farming has gotten a lot more technical in this day and age."

Pam and Tom have some later plantings that can be mechanically harvested. But for most of their vineyard they hire a labor contractor to bring in crews for picking, as well as for pruning and planting. "Probably one of the greatest things we've gained through this whole project is a great respect for the Hispanic culture," acknowledges Tom. "We've been amazed at the agricultural know-how these people have. No wasted motions, good attitudes, and when they are done the tools are cleaned and put away. And Demitrio Campos, the contractor, is amazing in how he makes sure that he puts the right amount of people on the job so that everyone makes enough money but there are enough people to get the job done in time."

For their second planting, they added Tempranillo and Cabernet varietals. "The Cabernet was basically just to prove that it could be grown here, because people said it couldn't," Pam says with a smile. A few years later they increased their acreage of Viognier. They also added just a half-acre each of Petit Verdot and Cabernet Franc, to be used mostly for blending.

Capay Valley Vineyards used to take their grapes elsewhere, but are now making all their wines onsite. They do have a winemaker who works out of Santa Rosa, but Pam and Tom are basically in charge of the harvest and the crush. "I'm the one who puts in the nutrients and the yeast and gets it all started," states Pam. "Then if I

get into trouble, I call the winemaker. I'm on the phone with her a lot during harvest time." Pam also does some of the testing but sends some things to the labs. "I go out and take cluster samples and check PH and sugar levels to see when to harvest. Pretty good for not ever having chemistry in school!" Pam is the one who's out there checking on the grapes, and she reports to Tom when something is broken. They seem to make a good team.

"There's the farming, the production of the wine, and then there is the marketing, which is the hardest one of all," says Pam with a chuckle. When they started, the idea was to hire a winemaker and make the best wine possible. Over the years, Pam and Tom realized that "the snob market is very small." They decided to work on good quality wine that's affordable and appeals to a larger audience. "Some people in the wine industry want to sell a few special cases for $200 a bottle, but you can't eat that way," affirms Tom. "Early on, we had a consultant price our wine, and we thought to ourselves, *We wouldn't pay that much!* That was the secret; if we wouldn't pay that much then we didn't think anyone else should."

Pam and Tom believe that finding a niche is an ongoing thing. They know they have to adapt and not just do the same thing, because customers are always on the lookout for something new. "Sparkling wine has been a good one for us. It's paid the bills," says Tom. "When you can see pallets being sold, then you know you've got something."

They were always very conscious of the label and the presentation. Instead of putting up a family name, they knew they wanted to evoke the region. So they chose the name Capay Valley Vineyards, and designed a golden line to represent the silhouette of their local hills.

During their initial research phase, Pam and Tom got the idea that they might be able to establish the Capay Valley as a federally recognized American Viticultural Area (AVA). AVAs add a level of distinction to winery labels, and let the customer know that at least 85 percent of the grapes in the bottle are from a specific region. They waited until they had some experience and some wine to show for their work, then they began the petition.

"It was a process," Tom says emphatically as he leans back in his chair, ready to tell the story. "We did it on our own without hiring any legal help. We just kept filling out the forms and sending information about our climate and soil back to Washington. It took a couple of years and during that time we learned that there had been grapes grown in this valley before, and that in 1861 a Capay Valley winery had been named "the finest vineyard in the state.""

The critical point that the Alcohol and Tobacco Tax and Trade Bureau wanted Pam and Tom to prove was whether Capay Valley was a distinct geographical area. "We seemed to be going round and round about this, and one day I said, *To hell with it; I'm sending them this relief map in a box.*" Tom pointed to the same map on the wall, made of plastic, showing the hills and indentation of the Capay Valley. "And after that, no more questions; we got the AVA."

Pam and Tom both acknowledge that the vineyard project has been quite an undertaking. It's been a steep learning curve. But Pam says she loves the satisfaction of pouring the wine and knowing that she touched every plant out there and was part of the whole process. Seeing their wine in Costco, next to all the other brands, they look at each other and say, "Hey, this is one heck of an accomplishment!"

Photo credit Lior Zilberstein

FULL BELLY FARM

FARMING MODEL: ORGANIC FARM, MULTI-FAMILY PARTNERSHIP, S CORP.

STARTED IN: 1985

OWNER: FULL BELLY FARM, INC

SIZE: 425 ACRES

MAIN CROPS: DIVERSIFIED FRUIT AND VEGETABLE CROPS, AND MORE

Every Monday morning for over twenty years, the partners of Full Belly Farm have met for their business meeting. They might walk or ride a bike through the fields to one of their private residences, such as Judith's straw bale house, or they might meet at the office building in the middle of the farm, newly built out of reclaimed redwood. They live and work together on the farm and though they each have different backgrounds and personalities, they all seem to have the unending work energy that it takes to make a small farm successful. Full Belly Farm is always a vibrant place, with trucks going up and down the driveway past rainbow fields of vegetables and flowers, sheep, chickens and cows being tended to, and happy polli-nators buzzing in the hedgerows. Judith is quick to remind me that, "to our eyes, the farm looks like a million projects that we can't get to."

The four long-time partners, Dru and Paul Muller, Judith Redmond, and Andrew Brait, are all incredibly driven in their passion about organic agriculture. As young people, they viewed farming as a way to change the world. Through their hard work they have made a difference, creating the roots of a deep revolution. Their success was a matter of hard work and good timing. It all came together when husband-and-wife team Paul and Dru took the risky step of looking for land and business partners.

Paul Muller grew up in nearby Woodland, on a commercial farm that grew primarily cereal grains and alfalfa. Friends know him as a practical philosopher, earning him the nickname 'Pastor Paul.' As a teen he worked on the family farm where he took part in the application of chemicals, and began thinking about their hazardous effects. A few years later he went to work for Outward Bound. "We were buying all the food for these kids in Safeway and then taking them out and teaching them self-reliance in the wilderness. I realized there was something about this that didn't make sense. To teach self-reliance I felt we might as well teach farming, because someone was working in the fields to get us that food. So I decided to go back into farming."

Paul was experimenting with organic farming when he met his future wife, Dru Rivers, who was working at the UC Davis Student Farm. Dru is one of those women with a small stature and a big presence. She came from Vermont and had a passion for growing and preserving food. "I knew from my high school days that I really wanted to somehow grow my own food, or be actively involved in that. It was also just part of the times in the 1970s; there was this whole movement of people going back to the land and homesteading."

Dru and Paul started farming together in Woodland, leasing several five- and ten-acre parcels, but it was about a twenty-mile round trip to get to all of them. Paul also noticed his broccoli had yellow spots due to pesticides that were floating in the fog. So they began looking for a bigger place where they could live and farm, and one that offered a higher watershed with fewer nitrates in the well water. Still, Dru acknowledges that when they got the lease on an old dairy and almond farm in Capay Valley, "It was a crazy idea that we would move and farm up here. We did all the things you are not supposed to do in the first year of business—we got married, had a baby, moved to a new place, and I quit my other job."

That first year they made plenty of mistakes, such as trying to harvest a few acres of walnuts by hand. "We thought it would just take a few hours to knock the nuts down with sticks," Dru recalls. "But after the first day we still had more than half the orchard to do, and our backs were so sore. The next year we hired the shaker trucks." Of course they are still making mistakes, experimenting and learning. Recently they lost several acres of newly planted asparagus, they just couldn't combat the Johnson Grass in that new field.

Soon after landing in Capay Valley, Dru and Paul started selling at the Palo Alto farmers market. They also started one of the early Community Supported Agriculture (CSA) programs, offering weekly boxes to subscribers. Full Belly Farm currently distributes about 1,100 boxes weekly to families as far away as the Bay Area and Sacramento. They have always put a focus on creating a beautiful presentation of local produce, and feel that the CSA helps bring people a greater connection to their local foodshed. As one of their customers put it, "It's like getting a veggie Christmas present every week."

When Dru and Paul were given the option to purchase the 100-acre farm, they were nervous about being able to afford it on their own, so they began entertaining the idea of taking on business partners. They reached out to their friend Judith Redmond and her husband, who were farming in nearby Winters.

Judith had studied plant science at UC Davis and had come to the conclusion that organic farming would be a good place to create change in the world. As it turned out, she was also a clear communicator, skilled at formulating agreements and getting them in writing, something Paul acknowledges as crucial to their partnership. The friends agreed that the land ownership would be kept separate from the Full Belly Farm business. This was helpful for tax and liability reasons. The farm business would lease out land from the partners and from other landowners in the valley.

As they formed their business partnership, they all discussed what would happen if they faced any of 'The 3 Ds': Divorce, Disability, or Death. "It's important to talk about any possible difficulties while you are all happy and wanting to be together," Judith says with a sage smile. "Then you have a plan to fall back on during hard times." They began farming together, and after a long process they finally bought the land in 1989.

Full Belly Farm took on another business partner in 1993. Andrew Brait came from a suburban Pennsylvania background. As a teen he developed an interest in rural life, and from the first day of his internship on a farm in Vermont he was committed to becoming a farmer. He came to Full Belly as an intern in the winter of 1990, and felt a close kinship with the people there. Andrew returned to Full Belly in the summer of 1992, and was offered the possibility of becoming a partner.

"We have similar values, and we've been working together a long time," explains Judith. "But you have to want to make it work, just like any relationship. A farm takes so much effort and time—it sure wasn't easy to make it what it is today. And if one of us abandoned, it could all go downhill very quickly. If we stopped taking care and upgrading systems, in a very short time it would collapse."

"Yes," agrees Paul. "It's a very human process. Sometimes we don't get along," he says with a chuckle. "But having that combination of skills is great. You have to understand that what you're doing is for a bigger picture, but you also have to be grounded. You have to walk on both feet. It's also been healthy for all of us to know that it must work financially. There's no Plan B, such as a rich relative. And we've been fairly cautious. We've grown as we're able to grow, but it's been by consensus, by and large. And in that, I think we've avoided some of the pitfalls that other farmers have faced. And I think we've probably learned from some of their lessons."

In retrospect, their big break came when a small-time chef named Alice Waters came looking to purchase baby lettuces for her Berkeley restaurant, Chez Panisse. "There weren't a lot of fresh-to-market growers at that time," explains Judith. "The niche market for baby lettuces found us; we weren't as good at marketing back then."

Photo credit Hannah Muller

Full Belly Farm has grown organically, meaning it didn't all happen at once. One reason they were successful is that they were all willing to make sacrifices. For many years they worked seven days a week. Judith worked another job for the first few years, commuting to Davis while holding meetings on a huge mobile phone in her car, then driving market trucks, and unloading late at night.

They have taken their time with making capital improvements, paying as they go and trying to stay out of debt. The land and buildings on the old dairy farm needed a lot of work. The original farmhouse was falling apart when the Muller family moved in. They renovated it one room at a time over many years, during the slower winter months. The Mullers still laugh about how one time someone sat on the toilet and the floor caved in underneath them. Both Judith and Andrew lived with their families in small rustic outbuildings for several years. Andrew and his wife eventually bought adjacent property with a modest pre-fabricated house, and moved in with their two boys. He exclaims, "I don't know how we did it, living in that tiny building smack in the busiest part of the farm for that long!"

Full Belly Crew and Owners

Full Belly also took their time hiring employees. "Again, people just found us," Judith recalls. "Some of the Jacobo family came to the farm and asked if we were hiring, then gradually they invited their family and friends. Many of those people still work for us today and have become crew managers." The Farm now has about eighty employees, most at full-time, with a few seasonal hires and some part-time office staff.

Besides vegetables and fruit, the farm sells meat and eggs. Early on, Dru began to grow flowers for sale, even though at the time Paul wondered if it would be worth their time financially. Dru also took the initiative of adding animals to the farm's crop rotation. The sheep and chickens move around the farm, eating vegetation left after produce has been harvested, and adding vital fertilizer to the soil. Soil health is very important to the partners at Full Belly. They grow cover crops to protect and amend the soil, and buy literally tons of compost and gypsum to apply before each new planting.

Full Belly Farm still goes to the same three markets as in the 1990s, but they now produce a greater variety of products. They have branched out to offer some processed items such as flavored almonds, milled wheat flours, almond butter, wool yarn, and sheepskins. With this diverse model, they may not be as efficient as if they were growing fewer things, but Judith likes to point out how this can have other benefits. "Diversity can equal chaos, but then we also have more avenues to fall back on, a benefit that is different from efficiency. It's good for our CSA to be able to offer that diversity, and it makes for nice displays at farmers' markets to have so many different things. We are also meeting another goal of sourcing our whole diet and creating local sustainability."

Educating the public and working toward policy changes have been other goals at Full Belly Farm. As part of their shared goal to advance sustainable agricultural policies, the partners have each taken on volunteer positions outside the farm, working on boards such as Community Alliance With Family Farmers, the Marin Farmers' Market board, the Ecological Farming Association, and the Yolo Land Trust. Full Belly Farm also hosts many visiting agriculture researchers. "There's a kinship and a bond that we all share as we do this work," explains Paul. "We keep getting affirmed that there are healthier ways to do things. We've been really lucky that we've had some amazing partners who have been very generous with their own beliefs that working together is the way you can get things done. It's that belief and that drive that has helped infect our kids. They were a part of it from early on and they now see that there's a place for them." Remarkably, all four of the Muller children have come back to live on the farm as adults.

Dru began leading field trip tours for school groups when her oldest children were in elementary school. "When kids from the city started coming here and really enjoying themselves, our own children began to realize that living on a farm was a special thing." After tagging along with her mom on those school tours, when she was sixteen years old Hallie Muller decided to start Camp Full Belly. The summer camp has grown into a thriving business with about 220 children coming each year to experience life on the farm.

Thousands of people also come to Full Belly Farm for the annual Hoes Down Harvest Festival. The festival is a harvest celebration extraordinaire, with hands-on activities such as felting and pizza making, circus shows, and music. It started as a fundraiser for the Ecological Farming Association, and now benefits over fifty local organizations as well. Hoes Down has been an important way to build community in the Capay Valley and beyond.

When Dru and Paul's son Amon took on the role of sourcing the festival's food and overseeing the kitchen, he became inspired. Now he and his wife Jenna run Full Belly Kitchen, from which they make value-added products from farm produce, such as pickles, jams, cookies and even bone broth. They also host events and cater dinners with almost exclusively local food. Their menus showcase the season's finest produce, with delicious dishes such as butternut crostini with pomegranate seeds and chèvre. As Amon and Jenna put it, "We find it so incredible that we can grow and produce everything that we need right here, except for coffee and chocolate."

The Full Belly Farm partners seem to understand that there is great value in just sharing the farm. Judith sees it this way: "We have this beautiful farm and it's really just value added to share what exists here in different ways. The Farm can now act as the marketing arm; campers know us thru our CSA and markets. Long-time customers want to come for a farm dinner at the Kitchen, or have us cater their events."

Recently, the Full Belly partners decided to incorporate, adding Amon and Jenna Muller as partners. Rye Muller has taken on the role of general facilities manager for the farm, and the Muller's youngest daughter, Hannah, has now started a full-fledged organic floral design business with the flower fields that her mother had started for farmers' markets years ago. Today, flowers account for over twenty percent of the farm's income.

The story of Full Belly Farm's early success also includes a bit of good luck.

There were very few organic farms at that time. Dru reflects, "People were questioning. There were so many things going on politically, and people wanting change. Part of the success of our business was timing. We started our farm at a moment in history, really, when the whole food movement was questioning chemicals, and the hard green tomato. We were at the right place at the right time. And that, to me, is just a little bit of karma or luck or whatever you want to call it."

But Dru also agrees with Paul as he points out the flip side of that. "There was a lot of determination. I would say that it was an evolving consciousness, and we were part of it, but there were a lot of meetings, and a lot of learning. People were cobbling ideas together about how to do it better, and really amazing teachers emerged. There were people who were way out front in entomology and asking the right questions. They were lonely voices at the University who now found an audience. Things like the organic food movement didn't happen because of folks with resources and the wherewithal to fund the kind of democratic technologies that many of us believed in. They didn't fund that because there was no money in it. It was self-taught. It was people believing something could be different and going out and trying to prove it, without a lot of sanctions. And it can still feel like we are fighting an uphill battle now, dealing with those who think that genetically-modified crops are the only way we're going to feed the world."

Walking in the shade of pomegranate trees filled with hidden birds' nests, past rows of bright flowers and green vegetables, it's obvious that farming is clearly a devoted act of right livelihood for the partners at Full Belly. "You know," contemplates Paul Muller, "the garden of Eden never disappeared. If you're humble enough, you can be part of its manifestation. Maybe not its creation, but its manifestation. There are times when I'm working outside and it's just all so beautiful, and I'm just really pleased with how I've enabled an expression of that beauty. I'm humbled to know that I am responsible for it. That's what true stewardship is. And you know, Wendell Berry calls it a revolutionary act, producing food this way."

SEASONAL LABOR

BY JUDITH REDMOND

Seasonality is a characteristic of agriculture. Some seasons are busy, others less so. Harvest time is fraught with urgency, the crop must be in the barn and out of the rain, or at the processing plant and out of the field, in a short window of time, or it will be lost.

Busy times mean more employees — and less busy times – well, seasonality in farming is why it has always been hard for farmworkers to find year-round steady work. Most people still think of farmworkers as migrants, moving from one part of the country to the next, following the harvest as crops mature. For migrant farmworkers from time immemorial, there have always been periods of time when work is scarce.

That popular conception, of farmworkers as migrants, isn't in fact, accurate any more. The number of farmworkers who migrate within the U.S. has fallen by 60 percent since the 1990's, just as migration back and forth from Mexico has fallen. Now, as documented by agricultural economists, only a small percentage of farmworkers migrate within the U.S. and this is true for both undocumented and documented workers, and in all areas of the country, in all demographic groups. There are several reasons for these changes at the macro level, and one is that the agricultural workforce is now older, more experienced in farm work, putting roots down in communities where their kids are in school, and they are less willing to migrate. Another important part of the changing picture has to do with immigration policy. While there are still workers moving in and out of the country from Mexico and Central America, that flow has diminished. In our Capay Valley, we have seen all of these factors at work.

It has always been an important principal at Full Belly Farm to provide year-round employment for a core group of employees. I looked at the trends from the past ten years of Full Belly labor records and noticed that there has been a steady, slow increase over the years in the number of people that we have on payroll in January. These are the core employees that stay through the winter, and their numbers have grown as the farm has grown. But every year, we prepare for the summer, starting in April, by bringing on new employees, and we have had a harder and harder time doing so in the last few years. We always hire on some summer high school students that can work a few days a week, but the full-time workers that we need to help us in the busy and critically important summer season, have been harder and harder to find. This means that fields and crops are left untended. I compared two years: 2011 and 2016, and noticed that we have actually been adding fewer people to our staff each year, and that certainly hasn't been because we haven't tried. These are trends for us to ponder, because the ag. economists are saying that they aren't going to change.

Of course, we would like to even out the seasonal changes in our labor needs, just keeping the core group of workers, without having to hire on additional summer help. But that is a wish that flies in the face of agricultural reality. We add additional people to our staff because there is work to be done from daylight to 'dark-thirty' (a term that we use in the summertime when we find ourselves loading trucks and printing invoices when we should be getting ready for bed). For example, in 2011 our employees worked almost twice as many hours (total, for the whole crew) in June as they did in January. In 2016, even though our workforce didn't increase proportionately, the total employee-hours worked in June was almost 2.5 times more than in January. That's what "seasonal" means at ground zero! The number of hours in a week gets stretched to capacity, farther than you thought was possible.

Sometimes you might hear farmers saying that they think agriculture is 'different' from other industries. This seasonality in labor need is one of the differences. There aren't as many farmers now as there used to be, so the urgency of bringing in the harvest and the need for additional labor at that time, is no longer a shared responsibility. Each farm will face these challenges alone, and find solutions (or not) that work for their unique conditions. The question that remains, for policy makers and for communities that value local food, is do we value our local farms enough to share the challenges and find solutions together?

This is an abridged version of an article that appeared on the Full Belly Farm website on Oct. 17, 2016.

GRUMPY GOATS FARM

FARMING MODEL: ORGANIC ORCHARD

STARTED IN: 2008

OWNERS: PAMELA MARVEL AND STUART LITTELL

SIZE: 20-ACRE PARCEL

MAIN CROP: OLIVES

Pamela Marvel and Stuart Littell planted their first rows of olive tree seedlings in 2008, as a retirement project. They had just bought a flat piece of ground alongside the highway that was bare except for a well, a new modular home, and a large metal storage shed. In only a few years Grumpy Goats Farm had already won a Gold medal for their organic, extra-virgin olive oil, awarded by the California Olive Oil Council (COOC). A bottle of their golden oil is easily recognizable by the goat on the label. There are no goats on the property; the name Grumpy Goats Farm is just a reference to the two of them stubbornly butting heads as they make decisions. Yet when you look at all they've accomplished in a short time, they seem to make a good pair. Despite their successes, they have also had plenty of surprising challenges.

Pamela has worked primarily in the tech industry, and Stuart owns his own construction company. Pamela always knew one day she would want to go back to the country life. "I grew up on a dairy farm. My parents always told us to study hard, get good grades, go to college, and don't go into farming whatever you do! So I listened to them and got a good job that kept me busy.

"But about ten years ago I said to myself, If I'm going to move to the country I need to have a plan." So Pamela started studying, taking Extension courses, and thinking about what she wanted to do. "The more I learned, I became attracted to the idea of olive oil because while olive oil is simpler than wine, it's still very much an art, and also a science. You're selecting the varietals and making decisions about what soil you can put them in and then you make decisions about the water that you give them, how much, and when? When do you pick them, early or late? So that seemed interesting."

Pamela began putting together a business plan. She tried working on it in her spare time but found she wasn't making much progress, so she decided to take six months off work. "Stuart was very supportive. It was not his dream, but he's been very supportive." In the process of researching her business plan, they began looking at different properties, trying to get an idea of how much land was going to cost, and what the costs would be to develop it. Pamela's research led them to Capay Valley.

"We found a piece of land in Capay Valley and said, *Ooh! This is the place!*" On the spur of the moment, they decided to buy. "It met our primary condition that it had to have the right kind of soil. Second, it had to have a good water supply—good clean water. Third, it had to have a good community; people that we could learn from. On top of that, this place is close to UC Davis."

The thing that ranked the lowest for Pamela and Stuart was the farmstead: the house, barn, or outbuildings. "What we got in that department was really pretty awful. So that's a development project. It's still not top priority."

Pamela and Stuart were smart to start small. They were going to start with planting only five acres, but at the last minute took the advice of their advisor to make more space for the Coratina variety they had chosen. They work with an agronomist out of Napa who advises them on everything, including nutrients, water, and irrigation.

"She was the one who said, *I've been talking to my Italian counterparts, and those trees that you have chosen, they're very precocious. They'll grow fast and big, you should give them a little bit more room.* We ended up with thirteen feet between trees, eighteen feet between rows. It was smaller than that before, so when we made that new matrix, oops, all of a sudden instead of taking five acres, we were taking eight acres."

They took a truck over to McEvoy's in Petaluma and bought tree seedlings in gallon pots. Then they got local help to prepare the land and put in the trees. Soon after, they extended some rows. And then, after year two in the spring, they faced their first big challenge.

"We had a big problem with field mice and voles," recalls Pamela. "There was a big outbreak of them here in the valley because of a very wet spring, which made ideal habitat for them. They came and chewed the bark, killing some trees. We had to replace about a third of our trees!"

Despite that loss, by 2010 they had enough fruit for their first harvest: a ton of olives equaling about forty-five gallons of oil. "That's what the agronomist meant by *the Coratina is precocious.* It grows fast!" extolls Pamela. Walking amongst the silvery green trees, I couldn't tell which were younger.

Grumpy Goats Farm now has six varieties of olives. The Coratina is almost three quarters of their orchard, and Piqual is another third, but then they planted Pendolino as a pollinator and they experimented with a few rows of Barnea, Nocellera, and Itrana. "The Barnea has been a complete bust. We thought it would do so well here, but it didn't like our place at all. Maybe it's that we have too much clay in our soil?" Pamela bends down and digs her fingers into the soil, bringing up a clump that when squeezed, holds its shape.

By some mix-up, they also ended up with Lecchino, which they did not order, but which are producing well. Pam has to ribbon off those trees and make careful decisions about when and where to use them, because in order to sell certified extra-virgin Piqual or Coratina oil, the yield must contain less than ten percent of other varietals.

Pam keeps the records, pays the bills, and does field work such as irrigation and pruning. She has put in hedgerows with native plants to encourage native bees and pollinators. Stuart's skills are in building things and taking care of machinery. "We collaborate on decision-making. Stuart is usually the one that pushes us to try something new. He has much better marketing instincts." They hire part-time help for certain jobs, but are still too small to cover consistent labor costs.

Looking into the storage shed, I see a small tractor, tools on the wall, and loops of drip tape on the ground. A year in the life of Grumpy Goats Farm includes plenty of weeding throughout the spring and walking the irrigation lines every couple of weeks during the summer, to make sure every emitter is dripping where it should be. There is liquid fertilizer to put in tanks that send it out through the irrigation lines. Additionally, in the summer they proactively spray every week or two, to combat olive fruit fly damage. Then comes the mad rush of harvest time in the fall, and marketing the oil in the winter. They sell about a third of the oil at farmers' markets, about a third wholesale, and about a third is sold through direct, mail order sales.

"The most effective marketing practice we've used is entering these olive oil competitions and having the good luck to get noticed, win some awards, gold medals, silver medals, and get a best of show. But I have no illusions," concedes Pamela. "This is early stages of olive oil competitions. I don't know how many hundreds of olive oil producers in California could soon become competitors."

Pamela tells me one story of a marketing blunder, when Grumpy Goats Farm spent the first two months of one year working with Williams-Sonoma. In order to sell with that name-brand company they had to learn about different online supplier systems, create *Best Before* date stickers, and have specialty cardboard boxes made to order. They sold a few cases, then Williams-Sonoma changed their policy and Grumpy Goats found they could not meet their demand for 160 cases of oil at a time.

In addition to watering, weeding, and harvesting there are tests to be done, records to keep, and certifications to uphold. Pamela gets animated when she talks about all this. She seems to enjoy the challenges of farming as a scientist would. She has done a fair amount of research and has spent time putting information on their Grumpy Goats website to educate consumers on the science.

"We take a leaf sample every summer and send it off to be analyzed to tell us what nutrients we might be low or high on. Our leaf sample analysis the last three years have shown some deficiencies. We have been trying to stay on top of that with fertigation."

In order to be certified as extra-virgin olive oil, there are several steps. First the oil has to pass lab tests to check the peroxide value and amount of free fatty acids. Several UV Absorbance assays are performed as well, and the ranking has to be lower than a certain level. So Pamela sends oil samples to a lab each year. Then those lab tests go to the California Olive Oil Council, which is a marketing industry group in the Bay Area with a tasting panel. The tasting panel looks for any defects in the oil. If it's undergone aerobic or anaerobic fermentation or if it's just gone bad, they can detect it. The oil must not have any defects in it and the oil must also have some positive aspects; it should have some fruitiness and some pungency to be ranked extra virgin. "If you pass that hurdle, you're allowed to put Certified Extra Virgin on your labels," explains Pamela.

One year, Grumpy Goats had a real puzzle with their Coratina. It was a low harvest and they only had ten gallons of oil. Still, they dutifully sent an oil sample off to the labs. Several days later they got a note back from the lab saying there were some unusual results. The Coratina oil had flunked one of the ultraviolet absorbency tests. The oxidation indicators were too high to be considered extra-virgin olive oil. "So right there, our oil was out," sighs Pamela. "We've learned to anticipate the worst and plan for it."

In addition to being certified extra virgin, Grumpy Goats is also certified organic. That's another layer of record keeping. "We have to be able to trace any oil sitting on a shelf in a store back to the field. From which field was it harvested? When was it milled? When was it bottled? So then if there was something wrong with the oil, we can start from there, tracing back. The way we do that is every time we take some olives to the mill they assign it a mill lot number. They assign that to the bucket of oil that is produced. And when we have it bottled at the mill, a bottling number is assigned to every bottle for that day, for that variety. Then when we sell the oil, I produce an invoice with our logging number on it. And so every bottle that goes out has a logging number."

Keeping all these records up to date can be a bit of a pain. But Pamela managed to get it down to three spreadsheets that satisfy her needs and that of CCOF. She has a field log where she records everything that is done on the field: mowing, pruning, fertilizing, weeding. There is a mill log with everything that happens at the mill, including the bottling. And then there is a sales log to record the outgoing of every single bottle, whether it's a gift, a sample, a purchase, direct marketing, wholesale, price per bottle, and any shipping costs.

And of course every business owner has to keep track of expenses, which is crucial at tax time. Applying for tax deductibles during the first years was especially important for Grumpy Goats. Pamela is clear: "My goal is to break even. Breaking even means just meeting the yearly expenses including the hired help, fertilization, harvesting, and property taxes. If I can earn ten grand a year I will be happy." There are a lot of unknowns to this. Olive growers throughout California will have to see where the price of olive oil will stabilize as this new market grows.

"We just need to keep it to one catastrophe a year. And maybe once in a while not have one," Pamela says with a laugh. Then she continues. "The whole farming thing, there's so much angst about it. But I like being outdoors, working in the orchard on a nice day. Making something grow and seeing in five or six years how much biomass you can actually produce is amazing. The farming is kind of a discovery. It's on the one hand like walking in a maze, trying to find your way to the center of a labyrinth. It's the challenge of what will it take to be successful as a farmer here? And unless you do it, you won't know."

WOMEN IN AGRICULTURE

Based on the interviews in this book, it seems that women play a prominent role in the farming profession. Eleven out of these fourteen chapters show women in leadership roles on the farm. There are the seasoned farm owners such as Trini Campbell, Dru Rivers, and Sally Fox, and there are the younger, up-and-coming women like Annie Hehner, Alexis Robertson, and Susan Muller. In 2015, Full Belly Farm held their first conference for female farmers. "Celebrating Women in Agriculture" was a well-attended event with over eighty participants from across Northern California.

Women in agriculture have been getting more media attention in recent years. In 2014, the USDA began focusing on women in agriculture, hosting roundtables and creating online resources. This may be in part to the 2012 Census of Agriculture, which found that almost a million women were working on farms, making up a third of the nation's farmers. However, less than a third of these women are principle operators or owners of the farms where they worked. The national total was actually down 2 percent from the 2007 census, probably related to the increasing age of farmers nationwide. Only 4 percent of women principal operators were under thirty-five years old in 2012.

The census also notes that the farms where women are principle operators tend to be smaller, with 82 percent of their farms being fewer than 180 acres, and 76 percent having sales of less than $10,000 in 2012.

Female farmers are more heavily concentrated in the west, southwest, and in tiny pockets of the east coast. Texas has the most female farmers of any state. Congratulations to those women of the wild west! Altogether, the census found that, "Women principal operators sold $12.9 billion in agricultural products in 2012, including $6.0 billion in crop sales and $6.9 billion in livestock sales. They operated 62.7 million acres of farmland."

https://newfarmers.usda.gov/who-are-women-ag
https://www.agcensus.usda.gov/Publications/2012/Online_Resources/Highlights/Women_Farmers/Highlights_Women_Farmers.pdf

LEAP FROG FARM

FARMING MODEL: SINGLE OWNER ORGANIC MARKET GARDEN

STARTED IN: 2012

OWNER: ANNIE HEHNER

SIZE: 20 ACRES

MAIN CROPS: TOMATOES, MELONS, AND SQUASH

Annie came in late for our dinner meeting with streaks of soil across her face, apologizing about needing to put in some irrigation. Annie is always busy and almost always smiling. She is a young woman with blond braids, who single-handedly runs her own organic vegetable farm. She told me she once worked a nineteen-hour day, harvesting, and said she was happy to do it because it meant she had lots of produce to sell at market the following day.

With only $6,000 that she had saved from one summer of working at another farm, Annie started Leap Frog Farm. She rents agricultural land from her parents, and pays a percentage of the property tax, as well as water pump costs. "I had to buy irrigation and tree seedlings," Annie recalls, "and lots of little supplies. I borrow a tractor from the neighbors. It's a great tractor that they never use, so I pay for maintenance, repairs, and it's essentially mine. There are so many unused tractors in this valley."

As a child she used to spend a lot of time at her best friend's home on Good

Humus Farm, though they never helped with the farming. "We just hung out and did arts and crafts. I never thought about wanting to be a farmer; I just knew I wanted to live where there were more trees." Annie's drawings of chickens and mandolins still adorn t-shirts sold by Almond Blossom Arts and Crafts. She never thought she would want to be a farmer, and after becoming one she never thought she'd grow salad mix, or go to markets in the Bay Area, but she's now learned to never say never.

While majoring in art at Humboldt State, Annie soon found that she couldn't afford to buy the organic vegetables that she wanted to eat. So she started volunteering at the Indian Health Services garden in return for free veggies. "I was just harvesting and weeding, but I really enjoyed being there, and I started imagining what it would be like to be a farmer."

The following year she got a job as head gardener at the Campus Center for Appropriate Technology in Arcata, despite having almost no experience. She just jumped in and learned as she went, which seems to be a common modus operandi for her. Through a lot of hard work and luck, Annie quickly became a knowledgeable farmer. She began helping a young couple with animal chores, working at 6 a.m. before going to classes. These friends helped her get a job at Neukom Family Farm after graduation. "I worked there for three years during the warm season—they had mostly peach orchards, tomatoes, and melons. The farm made their annual income during the warm season, so in the winter I would travel. I learned everything about farming while I was there. I saw them pull out acres of cherry trees and berry vines the first year because of the fruit fly. And I picked fruit till 9 p.m. and then got to see how appreciative people were at market the next day.

Annie admits that when she started Leap Frog Farm in Capay Valley, she didn't know how to farm winter things like salad mix, beets, or turnips. "I remember with my first batch of turnips I harvested, I was washing them each off in a bucket and then bunching them, thinking the whole time, *I know there's a better way*. Then I recalled one time when I was harvesting beets somewhere and we bunched them up first and then sprayed them clean." Annie laughs. "It only took me once to remember the right way to do it."

At first Annie planned to mainly grow things that stored well, like squashes, along with the obligatory tomatoes and melons that grow so well in the Capay Valley. She specializes in heirloom varieties and grows over twenty-five different varieties of melons alone. "I said I'd never grow salad mix, only head lettuce, because it seemed easier, but then one spring I brought some mixes of small greens to market and suddenly I became known for my salad mix. I don't even grow head lettuce anymore. I'm also known at the market for my radishes. Who would have thought, the lowly radish! Of course the cherry tomatoes are still my number one seller. I like introducing people to new things, like small rutabagas that you can eat raw in a salad."

She's glad to know that she doesn't have to grow everything. Annie often collaborates with Spreadwing Farm—they have better soil for growing peppers, so she takes their peppers to market and in exchange they send their interns over to her place when she needs help. Sometimes Annie holds work parties, and friends come to help with harvesting, planting,

or occasional big jobs like fencing. "But mostly it's just me working by myself. I have to be okay with things getting weedy." Indeed, the paths across Leap Frog Farm lead one through knocked down grass, and weeds creep over the cardboard mulch she has put around the young trees.

When Annie started Leap Frog Farm in the winter of 2012, she knew there would be a lot to do so she focused on infrastructure needs and decided to hold off on selling at markets until the summer. Meanwhile she organized a few work parties to build a straw-bale cooler to store her produce. Come springtime she found she had a few extra veggies ready to go, so she spontaneously looked up a market in Sacramento. "It was easy; things just started selling! I swore I'd never go to the Bay Area for market, thinking it's too far, but two years ago I had a lot of produce to sell so I applied to sell at markets in Marin and the first one I got into was the Country Town Market in Larkspur. It's an hour and forty-five-minute drive, not too bad, and the people there have been really great. I'm proud to say that after only three years I'm making enough to support myself and invest in my farm."

This investment included putting in new fencing, doubling the size of her farming acreage. The fence will stop the deer, and the added space will allow her to grow more row crops, which she first started growing in between her orchard rows. Annie has learned that being willing to spend money to save time and effort is a smart move. She first started drying mixed greens by putting them in a webbed bag and spinning it in the air above her head. "Finally I was selling enough that it made sense for me to buy a salad spinner from Johnny's Seeds, which cost $300. And it is worth every penny for the time it saves me. I made up the term "farma" one day; it's like karma on the farm, meaning that you get out of it what you put into it."

Annie says she finds it rewarding to be her own boss, getting to decide what needs to be done, when. Unexpected things come up all the time; Annie tells about fixing hoses for two hours even though a few days later she planned to install a whole new system. But those little plants needed to be watered right away. "My reward is going to the market, socializing with customers. Not everyone likes that part of farming, but I love it. I wouldn't want to just do wholesale or CSA deliveries."

You would think that since Leap Frog Farm is primarily a one-woman show, Annie would be too busy for much else. Yet Annie has been instrumental in starting the Capay Valley Farmer's Guild, the annual Sheep to Shawl event in Guinda, and the Seed Saving event. She has also taken over as the lead organizer of the myriad children's activities at the annual Hoes Down Harvest Festival held at Full Belly Farm. "When farming by yourself, you have a lot of time to think. So I think about how I can help build community." One wonders how she has time and energy for community organizing, requiring late night emails after farming all day. But she does it because she knows how important community is.

"I farm by myself, but not in isolation. I know that I'm in a great community of farmers and if I need help, it's there. I saw Rye Muller at the Farmer's Guild meeting and asked him to help me with putting hydraulic fluid in the tractor. He came over the next day. Now I know how to do it myself!"

MANAS RANCH

Farming Model: On-Site Farm Stand and Meat Market

Started in: 1979

Owners: Fred and Alice Manas

Size: 60 acres

Main Crops: Stone fruit

Today, when you drive into Capay Valley via Esparto, one of the first commercial buildings you might see is Manas Meat Market, with its red-and-white sign over wooden siding. The business caters to customers in more ways than one, offering a local USDA butchering facility for ranchers, and a tasty lunch spot with home-made sandwiches and pies. Another mile up the road, you can turn into the peach orchards of Manas Ranch to buy fresh fruit at the farm stand.

The market and ranch are the outcome of many years of experience and planning on the part of Fred and Alice Manas. When I ask Fred what he would call their model of farming, he says, "We call it Pray and Wish." Fred is a self-declared "hard-headed Spaniard", rarely seen without his cowboy boots and hat. His wife, Alice, a lawyer in her sixties, is presumably the tempering force in their business decisions.

They moved to Esparto in 1979, on twelve and a half acres of bare ground, which they quickly planted with peach and apricot trees. "My grandparents were fruit tramps," Fred explains. His grandparents came from Spain to Hawaii as indentured servants for C&H Sugar plantations. After working off their debt, they passed through San Francisco and settled in Yolo, working for different orchards. Eventually his grandfather started renting ground and farming on his own. When he passed away, he owned three ranches. Fred was raised on one of these, a three-hundred-acre ranch outside of Winters with 100 acres of apricots and about 150 head of cattle.

"I went to college. I couldn't wait to get off the ranch," Fred reminisces. "I studied thermodynamics and I met Alice. But when I moved to the city, I couldn't wait to get back to the country. I got a job at the University in Davis, where I oversaw all the heating and cooling on campus. Meanwhile we bought this place in Esparto, and I was driving the tractor at eleven at night."

They both worked full time off the farm in order to afford to farm. The first season they had fruit to sell, they put up a sign at the end of the road and an ad in the newspaper. Grandma and the two kids sold the fruit under a tree while Fred and Alice went to work. When Fred started growing stone fruit, he told Alice he didn't care if he had to dump the fruit on the ground; he was not going to sell it to a big company. His parents had lost hundreds of thousands of dollars as coop members of the canning group CalCan when the company suffered big losses over cyclamates, the artificial sweetener they were using in canned peaches. "Fred never forgot that, so that's why we decided to sell on-site," emphasizes Alice.

That first year, sales were good. The next year, Alice put out a guest book and had customers write in their address to get updates from the farm. "I sent out about three or four postcards each summer, letting people know that we were open and what varieties we were picking that month. Since then we've had a lot of repeat customers whom we got to know by name." Canners and jammers from the Bay Area or Lake County, where peaches don't grow, like to take a drive out to Manas Ranch and then go home and can together as a family tradition. "Sometimes people show up in RVs and take twenty boxes. It got to be that I was sending out about five thousand postcards at a time. The problem now is that the cost of postage has gone up so I just can't afford to do that anymore," laments Alice. "So I send emails, but it's not quite the same—not everyone likes to get another email."

As the Manases interact with their customers, they put a lot of intention into educating them. They found that people don't know that apricots can ripen off the tree and need to be a little green when picked, or they will get mealy. And people don't always understand about the different grades of fruit. "The first question I always ask," says Fred, "is, *What are you going to do with the fruit?* If someone says they are going to take it home and cut it up for something, then I encourage them to take those with blemishes, the seconds. The perfect fruits, the firsts, are just for setting in a bowl and eating from your hand." During harvest season, customers at the farm stand can watch through the window as fruit is brought in from the fields and sorted.

People will often ask Fred why their peaches aren't organic. "Let me find you one with a worm in it," he will tell them with tongue in cheek. "And they say, *I don't want one with a worm.*" Fred shrugs. He doesn't use any insecticides, relying on integrated pest management. "Good bugs eat the bad bugs," he says. But he uses fungicides to keep his trees healthy, and he doesn't want to deal with another layer of certification. "I'm already arguing with the USDA inspector," Fred laughs. "I hate to have somebody giving me orders."

Fred tells me that they might pick from each tree three times, minimum. He uses a refractometer to measure the sugar content of his fruit, and he says his picking crew can tell the maturity of a peach by eyesight. That is one reason he never considered opening a U-pick farm; there would be too much waste. He won't pick fruit with a 14-brix sugar measurement. "We wait, and then we will get fruit with over 20 brix. That's why we taste so much better than store bought."

With that high sugar content, Alice can make jams that take half the sugar of most recipes. Alice, who is originally a city girl from LA, learned to make jam from Fred's mother. It was a way to use leftover fruit that didn't sell. Now she has a trailer

Photo credit Tiffany Dozier

in the front yard that is a commercial kitchen, and she's making jam almost every weekend. "It's my quiet place," she confirms. "It's all prepped, so it's easy to just thaw the fruit and process it into jam." During the height of the summer Manas Ranch hires two students to work all day, peeling and freezing pulp. What Alice can't use—the pits and peels and any fruit that starts to go bad—goes to a friend who feeds it to his pigs. "When the pigs see the bin of peaches in the back of his truck, they come running and squealing with delight."

Fred has been a cattleman all his life. His family brought the first Black Angus into Yolo County. Originally, the idea for the butcher shop came out of the desire to process their own animals, which they did for a few years. "I've got my grandmother's chorizo recipe," Fred says proudly. He remembers his family butchering their own pigs every winter, making their own sausage and smoked meats.

Unfortunately, the drought years left the Manases with no good place to keep their cows, and the cost of buying hay was prohibitive—$300 a day for 250 cattle. "I thought he was going to have a heart attack the day we had to sell those cows," Alice reveals. "They were his pride and joy."

Now Fred Manas puts some of that energy into his role with the Farm Bureau. He sits on the Executive Council for Farm Bureau, as well as being on the Board of Directors. He is passionate about protecting the livelihood of farmers, and sees many new regulations as big trouble. "The thing is, whether you are small or big, you still have to follow the regulations either way. It's tough either way and California is just making it tougher and tougher." Fred references the Clean Water Act that requires farmers to pay a per-acre fee. And he is exasperated when speaking of a fifteen-dollar minimum wage. "My guys didn't ask for that! And overtime for farm workers! We have to keep our employees busy in the winter with little to do, then there is so much work in the summer and I can't afford to pay overtime."

Alice points out that every year there's a different challenge, whether it's not enough chill to set the stone fruit, or an early rain, or a freeze in late spring.

Fred adds with a grin, "That's how come we don't have to go to the casino; we gamble every day."

Fred and Alice took another gamble when they opened the Manas Meat Market in 2011. They had gotten some encouragement from several of the valley farmers and ranchers. Places like Riverdog Farm and Full Belly Farm wanted to take their meat to farmers' markets and restaurants, and the only way they could do that was with a USDA-certified butcher. The closest USDA facility was over a hundred miles away.

"We had the support of locals wanting us to do this," explains Alice. "We thought we could just go out and get a USDA loan. But we found out there's not so many banks that will even entertain the idea of working with the USDA." The Manases finally found a bank out of Texas to help them.

It took almost seven years for them to put the whole plan together. They worked with the Yolo County Farm Extension and Chico State. The original plan was much bigger than what they ended up with. Finding a location was especially challenging. "We looked at a place in Winters," Alice recalls. "We almost bought the train station in Esparto. When we bought this place, we had to go through all the regulations because we were applying to be USDA. We have a USDA inspector there almost every day."

They had to buy a sophisticated software program, which is designed to keep track of every cut of meat out of each carcass. When customers like Gillies and Alexis of Skylark Ranch come to pick up their meat, they get a printout. It tells them how many pork chops they have, how much sausage—everything they have by weight and number. Fred and Alice hired a butcher and a sausage maker. "The fellow who does our sausage used to work for Gallo. He's a sausage-making fool!" exclaims Fred. "I want to start putting up a hard salami. So that will hopefully happen in a couple of years."

The Manas Meat Market opened its retail store about a year after the meat processing facility opened. They bought all the equipment used, and started with the basics. The focus is on local production. They make sandwiches using their own bacon, pastrami, etc. Recently they started carrying cheese made from a local dairy, and a number of years ago they started selling their peach pies. An employee proposed the idea of selling hamburgers, so now once a week they grill hamburgers for lunch. "It's crazy," Alice remarks. "The highschoolers come over and we sell over two hundred hamburgers in two hours."

Fred tells me another story. "We have one long-time fruit customer from Santa Clara, from an Italian family. When we first opened the meat market, he went and tried some of our meat. Two weeks later he came up to get peaches and he had a big ice chest with him. He said, *Fred, we will never buy meat from the grocery store again.*" Fred maintains, "That's because our meat is dry aged. We let it swing in the holding room for a minimum of twenty-one days before we ever put a knife on it. Aging gives it its flavor, and its tenderness."

So far, the gamble on the meat market seems to be paying off. And Fred's determination will keep the ranch going. He admits, "It's hard to get a farm under seventy-five acres to be self-sufficient. You need about the same amount of equipment for fifty to a hundred acres as you do for five acres. Farming takes a lot of work, and you don't get paid much. You're pro bono, but you'll never starve."

He is not sure if their children will keep the farm going; they all have their own lives. Fred's son keeps telling him to cut down all the peaches and put in almonds, because they are less of a gamble in terms of weather conditions, and almonds require less spraying and lower labor costs. But Fred and Alice seem committed to their fruit orchards.

They both agree that farming is a lifestyle that they have chosen. "Friends don't understand why we are never available to go up to the lake to go fishing, or to go skiing." Alice shakes her head. "We don't have time for that stuff. Our priority is here. It doesn't feel like work. It's our sanity."

Photo credit Jonathan H. Lee

PASTURE 42

FARMING MODEL: PASTURE-RAISED LIVESTOCK AND DAIRY

STARTED IN: 2008

OWNERS: SUSAN AND KEN MULLER

SIZE: 32-ACRE PARCEL

MAIN CROPS: DAIRY, MEAT, AND OLIVES

The first time we slaughtered one of our own chickens, we had a book in front of us," laughs Susan Muller of Pasture 42. Susan and Ken Muller have largely learned off the cuff, navigating some giant learning curves. They now have a very successful farm and dairy, with green pastures sloping down from the hills on the western side of Capay Valley.

When I first stopped by the farm, Susan and her cousin were sitting on blankets on the lawn, serving three toddlers fresh milk and strawberries. It was an idyllic scene. But Susan says with chagrin, "I wouldn't recommend doing it the way we have. I wish we had done some more serious farming internships before we started on our own."

The young couple met while working at Nugget Market in Woodland. They got the idea to go traveling, and did spend three months volunteering on farms in France, through the organization World Wide Opportunities on Organic Farms (WWOOF). Ken had grown up in a farming family and they figured they'd like to give farming a try. Susan's mom had seven acres in Oregon, so in 2007 they moved up there with the idea of being egg farmers and raspberry growers. They invested $3,000 in the wrong type of berry for that region, but the egg business did well.

"In the beginning we didn't have enough product to sell at markets. We were just running through our small savings that we had saved up from other jobs. We spent all our savings while we figured things out—until we could start going to farmers' markets." Fortunately, Ken had planted olives in California with his father, Joe Muller, back in 2003. So by 2008 they had some olive oil to sell up in Oregon.

Meanwhile, Susan was pursuing her master's degree in Environmental Education at Southern Oregon University. Their farm plan has always included making time for school groups to come visit and participate in the collecting of eggs, feeding animals, and cooking with farm-fresh ingredients. While in Oregon, Susan and Ken hosted school field trips as well as overnight summer camps.

Soon their egg customers were asking if they had chicken meat for sale as well. Not long after that, Ken and Susan got a cow for themselves because, as Susan explains, "We realized that most of our grocery bill was going toward dairy products." With a cow on the farm, customers started asking if they had milk for sale, and so Ken and Susan started exploring the grass-fed dairy market.

Raw milk from grass-fed cows is thought by some to have health benefits. It can have higher levels of enzymes, vitamins, minerals, and essential fatty acids. Yet drinking raw milk also has a reputation for being a health risk. The dairy industry is a powerful lobby and there is a long history of legislation banning the sale of raw, unpasteurized milk. Many small conventional dairies have gone out of business, but despite that, those who are doing direct market sales (pasteurized or raw) are making a healthy profit.[2] So for Ken and Susan, it was just a question of how to sell milk directly to the consumer in a legal way.

As luck would have it, they met a neighbor at the farmers' market who had

2 (http://farmtoconsumer.org/news/news-24aug2008-2.html)

just given up their Grade A dairy license for their goat dairy business. Under that license, the state wouldn't let them sell raw goat milk or raw milk cheese, so in a dramatic move covered by the local press, these goat-dairy farmers burned their license. "When we met them," Susan says, "they were kind of evangelical about selling dairy as a herd-share operation, directly to the people without the state being involved. They came over to our place a few times and were very helpful as we figured out how to get our dairy business started. They turned us on to the Farm to Consumer Legal Defense Fund."

The Farm to Consumer Legal Defense Fund is a membership organization open to all farmers and consumers. Farmers who pay a membership fee have access to a group of lawyers via the Internet and phone. "They helped us type up our herd-share agreements. We didn't have to make those agreements up ourselves," explains Susan with obvious relief. "The organization is there to represent us, so if we are visited by state officials and we don't know what to do or say, we have an

800 number we can call for help. That makes us feel secure. Basically, in order to sell milk we just have to keep certain records, and we are not allowed to sell milk to the public at all."

In order to buy milk from Pasture 42, you first must buy a herd share. You are then the proud owner of a portion of a cow. In that way, the farmers at Pasture 42 are essentially contracted to take care of your cow and you are paying for their service, not the product. Any customer can buy meat and eggs directly from the farm, since these items are not under the same restrictive dairy license requirements.

Ken and Susan got into the meat and dairy business by listening to what customers wanted. "We meet the needs of a small group of vocal customers who want only 100 percent grass fed, as well as people looking for raw, organic milk." And some customers just appreciate that Pasture 42 is local and in several ways more sustainable than conventional dairy. Instead of buying grain that has to be shipped from the Midwest, they are growing everything that the animals need. Susan justifies that. "The cows may not give as much milk as in a grain-fed dairy but they still give plenty, and over time we can tweak our herd so that we keep the ones who do well on this diet." The cows on small dairies are healthier and live much longer than on conventional dairies, something like twelve years versus just forty-two months.[3]

Susan and Ken have already had to make adjustments to their herd, as they moved from Oregon to California. They landed in Capay Valley after a long search. In Oregon, they had grown to the point where they needed more land. "We were leasing small pastures and had to sometimes move cows across the road, which was exciting, if not dangerous, and not really viable long term." They looked in Oregon but couldn't find a place that was big enough and that also met other requirements. On a trip to visit family in Woodland, their uncle told them about a place that was coming available down the road from Full Belly Farm.

The property was already set up for livestock, done with a Natural Resources

3 (http://farmtoconsumer.org/cow-shares.html)

Conservations Services (NRCS) grant eight years prior. "We had spent so much time fencing in Oregon. This place on Road 42 was perfect for us because it was cross fenced and had water in each paddock. And there were some young shade trees already planted. There was also a livable house. It was exactly what we were aiming for."

Even this perfect set up required some adapting to. With just a ten-degree difference in average temperatures from Oregon, and similar rainfall, they had to change the forage crops. Where they used to rely on perennial pasture all year long, now it is too hot in summer and too cold in winter, leaving only two shorter periods of growth in between. It takes more effort to feed the cows in California, rotating between growing Sudan grass in summer and wheat in the winter. The cows tend to lose productivity in the heat, so Ken and Susan are experimenting with giving them more alfalfa to help with that.

Pasture 42 goes to three markets a week, and has several drop-off areas where customers pick up milk, eggs, and meat. They have about 1500 chickens at any one time, which they move around the property in large chicken tractors surrounded by electric fences. In addition to around twenty cows, they also have pasture-raised hogs for meat.

At the time of the interview, Ken and Susan are basically sharing a full-time position as business owners, while also sharing in the care of their two young children at home. "We are growing a business and a family," Susan says with wide eyes and a shake of her head. Doubtlessly, there is a lot of overtime involved. They are lucky to have some backup from their parents. Susan's mother, Margaret, has moved down from Oregon to be close to the grandkids. Grandpa Joe continues to help with the daily operations at Pasture 42, sourcing equipment and occasionally disking a field. They also rely on having the help of several interns year round. As hosts with MESA, Pasture 42 has had interns from as far as France and the Republic of Georgia. These young people become part of the community for a year, learning as they work. They feed the animals, milk the cows, plant feed pastures, move irrigation, and have even helped renovate the barn.

Susan feels like soon they will be ready to hire some regular employees. "But we want to hire ourselves full time first. With employees, we will have to get an Employer ID number and learn new paperwork—which is kind of daunting as I'm the one doing all the paperwork and outreach." For now it is a family-run business, with plenty of help from Grandpa Joe on the tractor and Grandma Margaret babysitting the children.

"It's a ton of work," says Susan. "But we are our own boss and we don't have to go to bed at night wondering if what we are doing is worthwhile. At least we know we are not having a negative impact on the planet. We feel we are making a difference on a small scale, by providing these products. When people are buying from us then they are not buying from far away or from where animals are mistreated. And we get to be outside, and have fun around the critters, and the kids get to grow up with a really cool experience of knowing where their food comes from."

THE LEGALITY OF FARMING INTERNSHIPS

Though we think of internships as a vital way to gain new experience in many fields (pun intended), farming internships are not always legal.

Farms have a long history of offering internships, usually involving a trade of hours of labor for room, board, and a small monthly stipend. For many people wanting to get into farming, internships or apprenticeships seem like a good way to start. Several farmers interviewed for this book got their start in farming via internships on working farms. Some of them, like Andrew Brait of Full Belly Farm, were city kids with almost no experience in farming.

But it is technically illegal for most California farmers to offer internships on their farm and some farmers have been sued for doing so. According to the Fair Labor Standards Act of the U.S. Department of Labor, any for-profit business offering internships must pay minimum wage and overtime, unless they can meet six requirements "similar to training which would be given in an educational environment."

The problem can be that most farmers don't have time to closely supervise and train an intern for the entire period of the internship, while the farm often does benefit from the activities of the intern, and the intern may displace a regular employee. But for small farms struggling to make a profit, paying an inexperienced worker minimum wage can be a real hardship.

One solution is for farmers to become hosts with agricultural training and exchange programs such as Multinational Exchange for Sustainable Agriculture, or WorldWide Farmers Exchange. Find out more at mesaprogram.org and worldwidefarmers.org.

Some of our own farmers from the Capay Valley helped put together a guide to clarify this issue for new farmers. See the California Farmlink guide at http://www.californiafarmlink.org/storage/documents/CA-Guide-update-3-2014.pdf

Trini Campbell with Tractor Operator Carlos Hernandez

RIVERDOG FARM

FARMING MODEL: FAMILY-RUN ORGANIC TRUCK FARM

STARTED IN: 1995

OWNERS: TIM MUELLER AND TRINI CAMPBELL

SIZE: 350 ACRES

MAIN CROPS: VARIED VEGETABLES AND FRUITS

Chickens and cats cross my path as I make my way to the small, refurbished old farmhouse that sits across the dusty driveway from the office and packing shed of Riverdog Farm. Latino music and laughter follow me down the path. Trini Campbell welcomes me into her modest kitchen, where freshly harvested lettuce, kale, and mandarins overflow on the countertops.

Tim and Trini were just kids out of college when they moved to California in order to work for Tim's aunt, who had a food purveyor business in Napa Valley. Tim had done an internship with the agricultural education program at Hidden Villa in Los Altos the year before. They were doing deliveries for Frank's Fresh Foods, picking up fresh goat cheese, edible flowers, and veggies and delivering them to restaurants.

By odd chance, one of the vegetable growers had to leave his two-acre field to take a job making a movie, so Tim and Trini started harvesting and marketing the veggies, getting paid by the hour. The following summer they proposed that they rent that same field, and so began their first farming operation. Trini recalls, "I have a picture of our first farmers' market and we just had fava beans, green onions, and green garlic on one little table. We started very small and just grew as demand grew."

As they became regulars at the farmers' markets, they made strong friendships with farmers from the Capay Valley. Jeff and Annie Main of Good Humus, as well as Paul Muller and Dru Rivers of Full Belly Farm, welcomed them into their community, discussing the weather, sharing farming advice, and looking out for one another. Tim recalls the time that young Allison Main suddenly disappeared one busy market day. "After we were all frantically searching through the market, I found her asleep in the back of her parent's delivery truck."

Tim and Trini kept their delivery route with Frank's Fresh Foods and that kept them in the loop about what chefs wanted, and gave them an instant market for their own produce. "From doing that delivery route we knew that there was demand from chefs for perfectly fresh produce. Freshness became our niche." Tomatoes have continued to be the mainstay of their fresh offerings, though they have greatly diversified. They now sell fruits, veggies, nuts, eggs, poultry, and pork. In addition to selling wholesale and at farmers' markets, Riverdog also delivers weekly produce boxes to customers who subscribe to their Community Supported Agriculture (CSA) program.

As we snack on mandarins and raw almonds, Trini tells me about a new project: Riverdog Farm is helping a company beta test a new solar chicken coop lighting system, which could increase the production of eggs while using less energy and keeping the coops mobile. "One of the keys to successful farming is adapting to new circumstances. We are always trying to improve, altering our systems so they are more efficient and not just assuming we can follow the same pattern as last year."

At first Tim and Trini stayed adaptable by working side jobs. They built gardens for chefs, and they managed other people's orchards. They used their limited in-

Tim Mueller

come to buy seeds and eventually started using their credit cards in lieu of loans to buy equipment. It was just the two of them doing everything for the first few years. It took five years before they made enough profit to quit the side jobs and farm full time on fifteen acres in Napa Valley.

In 1995, Tim and Trini became parents to a beautiful baby girl. That year they decided they had to move to Capay Valley if they really wanted to continue farming for a living and buy their own land. They had hoped to stay in the Northern Bay Area, but land prices were unaffordable for them. Paul Muller helped them find property with a house to rent in Brooks. They brought a handful of workers with them from Napa and started farming on thirty acres. "It was a rough transition year," recounts Tim. "I was commuting back and forth, keeping some of our farming projects going in Napa, and slowly moving all our supplies to Capay Valley."

"Doing everything ourselves, we really ran ourselves down," acknowledges Trini. "Hiring a few people really helped the farm grow and stand on its own. A lot of the people we've hired have come from agricultural backgrounds, so they have taught us things and really helped our operations." Even so, it was still over a decade more before Tim stopped working twenty-hour days, farming all day and then driving their delivery trucks at night.

Meanwhile, their daughter Cassidy grew up alongside the children of Riverdog's employees. "I feel like our employees are extended family," says Trini, who often offered these children homework tutoring in her kitchen. Now some of those same children, as well as Cassidy, come back to work on the farm every summer.

Eventually Tim and Trini were ready to buy their own land, and found sixty acres in Guinda. "This place didn't have much infrastructure," admits Trini. "Just a well and a tiny rundown house. We were lucky to have my parents give me part of my inheritance upfront—$40,000—to put as a down payment. That was a huge help. Then we still had to get a loan. We showed the bank all our records in Quickbooks, and we could show a pattern of growth. There are a lot of agriculture lending rates. We were lucky to have gotten a flexible interest rate loan right at a time when they were going down. So as we were getting ready to pay off our loan we were only paying 4 percent. And we bought this place right before the big real-estate bubble."

Riverdog Farm has grown into a decent-sized family-farm operation, owning about 350 acres and leasing another 150 acres. And with that growth comes a few challenges. Labor accounts for at least half of their expenses and as they have no HR department, it's up to the owners to keep up with current laws and to be effective managers. Trini explains one strategy of theirs: "Whenever we have a strong net income year, we do profit sharing and give everyone bonuses and time off. It's a perk and incentive for them to work harder during the year so we can all have a bonus and break at the end of the year."

Fuel is also a major expense, and one that can fluctuate greatly. "Food prices don't really go up, but our expenses do go up," explains Trini. "We are often checking to see if we are really going to cover our costs."

Maintaining layers of certification is another expense for farmers to consider. Having large wholesale accounts is one way that Riverdog Farm maintains their business. And those wholesalers require their farmers to have the new third-party certification of GAP (Good Agricultural Practices). This involves record keeping and a costly annual inspection. And then there is the organic farming certification. Riverdog does both of these certifications through California Certified Organic Farmers (CCOF).

Organic certification can be a headache, with continuous record keeping and a whole-day inspection once a year. Farmers have to schedule in time to walk the inspector around all the boundaries, show maps of the farm, and a list of all crops must be submitted. The process is also very expensive. "We pay about $10,000 a year for inspection. And they are not just checking about synthetic fertilizers and pesticides, but also checking on farm management practices. They want you to do crop rotation, cover crops, and soil enhancement practices. So for example they want to see your receipts and invoices to prove you bought the vetch to grow a cover crop."

Trini remembers when it was a lot simpler. "If you are just doing direct sales and have customers that trust you, you may not need the certification; you can just explain that you are following organic practices, and invite them to come see your operation. But for us, our wholesale customers demand the CCOF certification."

In 2015, Riverdog Farm was also looking at how to deal with changes in water availability. "I didn't really understand about all the changes we might have to deal with due to climate change," exclaims Trini. "It's not just trying to predict weather, but also predicting what kind of windfall might come our way and how we can tap into it. How can we get creative and keep our income while producing less water-intensive crops?" She was considering that they could offer services for

hire such as pruning, mowing, or ditch digging, making use of the heavy equipment the farm owns.

Tim interjected, "Being adaptable also means staying abreast of changing market trends. The heirloom tomato is not as exciting to consumers as it was a few years ago." He notes being grateful for accounts with companies like Blue Apron, at a time when more consumers are opting for menu delivery services.

One windfall seems to have come their way in the guise of an acquaintance asking if they had room to graze a few pigs. "This guy essentially abandoned these pigs on us," Tim tells me with a chuckle. "We had a few butchered and it dawned on us that we could get into the pasture-raised hog market. We commissioned someone to make some pork sausages, and boy did they became a hot item." Riverdog Hog has become well known in certain circles, and the farm was recently awarded a value-added producer grant from the USDA, which they will use to process their own sausage, ham, and bacon.

In addition to the challenges of farming, there is also the challenge of self-care. Trini mentioned the importance of setting aside time. She recharges by going on hikes in the hills, knitting, or cooking a special meal. "Some people are used to working five days a week and then having the weekend, but farmers don't always have the full weekend, and so daily nurturance can give you more stamina." For over twenty years, Trini has spent almost every Saturday selling at the Berkeley Farmers' Market. Working every weekend takes dedication, but she thoroughly enjoys seeing the same families every week. "I see kids who are growing up raised on our food, and it's just a really good connection."

In her personal time, she likes to enjoy the quiet of the valley. "I love being aware of the whole life cycle, paying attention to all the miraculous changes. I like seeing the blossoms and then watching how a tiny fruit will develop and eventually change into a ripening fruit. And seeing the bees doing their work and their legs full of pollen. It's all such an intricate system."

Photo credit Robert Durell

SEKA HILLS FARM & RANCH

FARMING MODEL: AGRIBUSINESS AND DIRECT MARKETING

STARTED IN: 2004

OWNERS: YOCHA DEHE TRIBE

SIZE: OVER 9,000 ACRES FARMLAND AND RANGELAND

MAIN CROPS: OLIVES, NUTS, AND VINEYARDS

James Kinter, Chairman of the Yocha Dehe (pronounced yo-cha dee-hee) Property, Farm & Ranch Committee, greets me outside the tribal offices in Brooks, California. He loosens his tie after a morning full of meetings. We sit outside, drinking ice tea and looking out over a central lawn and native hedgerow with pathways to the Yocha Dehe School and community houses.

James tells me that when he was growing up, this same property was planted in tomatoes and orchards. It became Tribal Trust land in 1940, after years of effort on the part of the tribe to acquire land suitable for farming in their own valley. The Rumsey Farming Association was established in 1938 as the tribe's farming collaborative. They grew corn and wheat on this parcel. After WWII, the tribe applied for loans for farming expenses, but couldn't even get veterans loans because they didn't legally own the land—it was only held in trust. So, during the 1960s the land was leased to other farmers.

James attributes his interest in agriculture to the fact that he grew up surrounded with farming as a way of life. "My mother worked in the fields as her first job; her parents and grandparents were farmers. And when I would go over to play at a friend's, it was usually on a ranch or farm. Before the casino, we all thought agriculture would continue to be the tribe's main endeavor."

The success of Cache Creek Casino has given Yocha Dehe the opportunity to reinvest and diversify. The tribe moved out of the HUD houses behind the bingo hall, and built the LEED homes and community buildings where James and I sit. "We bought the Davis Ranch next door as our first purchase," James recalls. "It was already planted in walnuts. We wanted to have a buffer so that was part of the reason we bought properties around where we live. But when we saw that we made good money on the walnuts, we soon bought other property and started to invest in agriculture, planting safflower, almonds, and olives."

I ask James if he has any words of advice for those who might be in a similar position: someone with wealth who wants to diversify into agriculture. He squints and says, "Well, three things come to mind. First you've got to make sure you do your research, you have to take a long-term view, and it's important to create partnerships. But we are different than the average ag-investor in that we have our trust land here, so we aren't just going to pull up and go somewhere else." James notes that just outside the valley, people had recently planted a lot of water-intensive nut orchards that they were trying to flip. "I think you have more of a long-term view, more care for the land, when you grow up on the farm and it's a family-run business."

In 2004 the Yocha Dehe Property, Farm & Ranch Committee was created. Fifteen members sit on the committee, which James admits is a lot. However, they have steering committees, like the Seka Hills Olive Mill steering committee, which has just five people and can be more focused. Only tribal citizens sit on the committees. They do have advisers come in; sometimes it's neighbors from the valley who help strategize on how to use the land in the best way. But that's becoming less needed

Photo credit Robert Durell

now as the tribal members become more knowledgeable. "We do our due diligence, researching and planning, talking to our neighbors. It's been a long and complicated endeavor. If you look at all the land that the tribe owns in the valley, you'll see that we tend to go above and beyond in our caretaking. We value the view-shed and we want to take care of the land like our people taught us to do. That's why we got into this."

A lot of the land the tribe owns in the valley was out of production at the time of purchase. One parcel they bought was an overgrown organic farm that had been out of production for several years. In partnerships with some of the local organic farmers, the tribe turned it into a productive, organically farmed piece of land. "We have great resources here in the valley, and I'm also thankful for having great neighbors. We partnered with the Barsottis on the organics; they taught us a lot as we split the cost and the produce, and they then marketed the produce. In organic farming, marketing is the most important part, and we didn't want to try

James Kinter and Jim Etters inspect the harvest.

and reinvent the wheel. It's been a great partnership." Yocha Dehe has also leased land to Riverdog Farm and done some collaborating with Full Belly Farm as well.

Farming is always a challenge, year to year, depending so much on the weather. James feels grateful for the local watershed, with allocations from Clear Lake. But even with a good water source, Yocha Dehe Farm and Ranch wants to focus on crops that are more drought tolerant than nuts, which is why they are happy with their olives. "We haven't had a problem with bugs like the olive fly, maybe because we are so dry up here. Our olives are not certified organic; we do spray sometimes, but still we think olives are better for the environment."

The property across the highway from the casino is mostly dry farmed, planted in safflower, wheat, olives, and almonds. There are also a few acres of grape vines out in front of the casino, which started out just as a landscaping, view-shed project. Then when they saw that there was a product on the vine, the casino took the first shot at making wine—a white Viognier and a mixed red. The casino management found it didn't have time to maintain that project so the Farm & Ranch took it on. With their farm and ranch employees, they've developed what they have today: an award-winning red blend.

"The employees that we have are great; we are so blessed to have them. Jim Etters, Dave Frikee, and Adam Cline — without those guys and the people that help them, our programs wouldn't be where they are. They implement all our plans. We didn't start out trying to get into the wine industry, but we got into it because the grapes were there and we thought we could do something with it. With only sixteen acres of grapes we are able to produce twenty-five thousand cases of wine a year, which is pretty good. We won second best of class for red blend in Napa. Napa has some of the best wine in the world so that was a real boost for us!" The tribe also has about five hundred head of Black Angus cattle. They are being careful not to overgraze, so they move the cattle to different parcels and plan to max out the herd at about 650 animals. The cattle are part of their land management plan to remove invasive species and prevent soil erosion. Most of the beef gets sold into the market for cash, but they do process some each year for tribal citizens to enjoy. "I like that it's free-range beef," says James. "When I cook it, it's just as tender as the grain-fed beef."

While they sell beef, nuts, wheat, and safflower on the open market, the tribe has recently started holding back some products for the Séka Hills label. ('Séka' means 'blue' in the tribe's native language.) James mentions plans to start selling their beef at the olive mill storefront. They currently have flavored nuts as well as honey, balsamic vinegars, and of course the Séka Hills olive oil and wine on the shelves. "We have a lot of products. Once we started diversifying and finding success with farming, we thought we'd see if we could do something like the olive mill."

A lot of research went into the Séka Hills olive mill. "That wasn't something we just decided on overnight. The first two years of olive harvest we crushed in Santa Rosa. Then we figured out that it made more sense to crush them right here and also provide the local community with a state of the art milling service." The 14,000-square-foot facility is definitely impressive, with the storefront featuring a floor to high-ceiling glass window view of the Italian mill just beyond the tasting room bar, and outside seating looking out on the blue hills. What's really impressive according to James is that, "In 2015, ten gold medals came out of our olive mill. Most of those were from Capay Valley, so that's something the valley can really toot their horn about."

James is excited to see how the olive mill helps to create further partnerships. "With farming, I feel like you can't do it on your own. Especially in a valley this size, because we don't have thousand-acre spreads, we just have maybe three hundred acres here and one hundred there. We are at a bit of a disadvantage compared to San Joaquin Valley, where people can put out these bigger quantities. So that's why we are kind of forced to think outside the box and work together. One way the almond growers here did this was by contracting with Mariani Nuts as a group, and thereby getting the trucking cost down."

Another example of collaboration occurred when James's mother, Paula Lorenzo, along with local farmer Dave Shearing came up with the idea for Capay Valley Vision (CVV). After some tense community relations surrounding the expansion of the casino, this organization brought together a diverse group of community members who work in task force groups to create community action plans around issues of Agriculture & Environment, Economic Development, Recreation, Housing, and Transportation. Together they have worked to preserve a unique sense of place, funded many feasibility studies, and created a Capay Valley Grown branding label. As James puts it, "Capay Valley Vision has enabled Yocha Dehe and the people in this valley to have meaningful dialogue. It's really changed the dynamic in the valley. We are neighbors; we shouldn't be fighting each other."

With a smile, James also notes that change is happening because his generation is taking over the tribal offices at the same time that local farming families are passing much of the work to the next generation. "These are people I went to school with; we have experience working together. So things in Capay Valley have really changed because of that."

The current goal for Yocha Dehe Farm & Ranch is to expand their Séka Hills label offerings of olive oil, wine, and flavored nuts. In the long term, they will keep researching and looking for different opportunities with crops that are drought tolerant and better for the environment. James reflects that, "Yocha Dehe is now the largest landowner in the valley, and we are happy about that. We want to help boost the community brand, so people come to know Capay Valley means great quality."

SKYELARK RANCH

FARMING MODEL: PASTURE-BASED LIVESTOCK RANCH

STARTED IN: 2010

OWNERS: GILLIES AND ALEXIS ROBERTSON

SIZE: 60 ACRES

MAIN CROPS: PASTURE-RAISED MEAT, EGGS, AND FIBER

Gillies Robertson stands out in the Capay Valley community. He's a lanky red-haired young guy with a curious accent. He left Scotland at twenty-one to go backpacking in Australia, and met Alexis there. Alexis is a California girl. She grew up in the town of Chico, where she says she "learned all the basics from having horses as a young girl." Gillies followed her to California in 2007, and they married in 2008.

Gillies and Alexis both graduated with degrees in Environmental Studies, focusing on resource and land management. This kind of degree usually leads to jobs within government, or consulting firms, private industry, or nonprofits. Resource management students often don't see eye to eye with livestock ranchers. So how did these two decide to take the leap and become ranchers rather than consultants?

Gillies puts it down to having read a lot of Joel Salatin books with titles like *The Sheer Ecstasy of Being a Lunatic Farmer*. One winter Gillies did an internship on a huge organic carrot farm in the central valley, and quickly decided vegetable farming

wasn't for him. But he and Alexis both knew they preferred to be working outside, and liked the idea of being their own boss. Alexis did her master's thesis on the reduction of star thistle (an invasive plant in California) through animal grazing. She researched the timing of impact and number of animals necessary to eradicate the star thistle, while not overgrazing the land. After doing this research it seemed like a natural fit, to use livestock as a land management tool and sell the meat that she and Gillies raised.

Without a lot of experience, they decided to venture out on their own. They did some informal work on farms in the Chico area, such as an olive orchard ranch with livestock that grazed between the rows of old trees. "We did a couple batches of meat chickens on other people's property, just to get a feel for it," says Gillies. They met some key mentors in the Chico area whom they credit with showing them the ropes. Then they just leapt at it. "We realized we could take this to the next level and not just do it as a hobby."

They registered with California Farmlink, and found sixty acres available for lease in the middle of Capay Valley. It had about twenty acres of old almond orchard, twenty acres of hay field, and twenty acres of hilly rangelands. They signed a seven-year agricultural lease and moved into an Airstream behind the main house. Soon afterwards, the house came up for rent. "We decided it would be worth the extra cost, not having to share the property with someone else who had other usage ideas," explains Alexis. "Plus with the house came the use of the barn, the shed, and conveniences like indoor plumbing and air conditioning."

The idea of farming on someone else's property can be challenging for new farmers. But for many, it's the only way to start. Alexis and Gillies seem happy with their decision. They have a good relationship with the owner and first right of refusal. "He's happy that we are taking care of the place, and maybe it's also lucky that he is out of state most of the year," Gillies quips.

Capay Valley has turned out to be a good central location for Skyelark Ranch. It's within easy reach of Bay Area markets, but any closer to the city and land prices would be too high. It worked out nicely that they are also in between Orland, where the pigs go for slaughter, and Dixon, where the lambs go. They have to get their meat slaughtered and packaged at USDA-inspected facilities so that they can sell directly to customers. If they used a state facility they wouldn't be able to do that. "It was very handy that Manas Meat Market opened up in Esparto the same year that we got here," recounts Gillies. "They do all our cut and wrap for us, and make our bacon."

They both kept other jobs at first. Alexis still works part-time from home with the Capay Valley Farm Shop. Gillies was working full time at the Resource Conservation District, doing biology study consulting work. In the summers he would go down to part time, to work more on the ranch. After just a few years of this they decided it was time for him to go full time on the farm. "The ranch was making enough income and trying to balance work on and off the farm was getting too crazy," Alexis remarks. "So far so good."

"We are doing this all dry farmed," points out Gillies. "The well here is not up to it, so that is a struggle and a challenge. We are trying to be as conservative as possible." California had been in a drought since they started farming. When their domestic well went dry in 2014, they found that one positive aspect of leasing was that the cost of the new well was on the landowner. But Alexis and Gillies had to deal with no water for six weeks in the middle of summer. There was an agricultural well they could use for the animals, but they had to fill a tank and drive it by truck to all the animals, twice a day. "It took so much time!" rants Alexis. "And we had two thousand ducks at that time. That was probably our biggest challenge—not to mention keeping ourselves clean."

As modern farmers, they found some help for their challenges online, such as YouTube videos of how to make a pig waterer that's not going to be destroyed immediately. "You can learn almost anything on YouTube," laughs Gillies. "And we are learning a lot from the diversity of farmers here in the valley, who generously share tips and resources."

The Skyelark herd started with twenty ewes of California Red sheep, which they inherited from a neighbor in 2011. California Reds is a breed developed at UC Davis that are born with auburn wool, keeping the red coloring on their face and legs. "We've had people advising us to switch to a different breed of sheep that will produce higher yields of meat, but we like the Reds so we plan to keep them and do both. We will just have to separate them for breeding time."

Alexis pulls out a bag of carded wool from the cupboard and shows me the fine pink strands hidden within the white fluff. They take their wool to the Yolo Mill for processing, and sell yarn, roving, and batting at the farmers' markets. "I love shearing," Alexis says with a giggle. "I know it sounds weird, but it's just a fun personal challenge. If I do it well it feels great; if not, it's a big struggle for me and the sheep."

Skyelark Ranch is a member of the Fiber Shed, a Bay Area network focused on developing local fiber markets for locally grown clothing. For a fundraiser event, Skyelark was teamed up with a clothing designer who knitted a "grass-fed top" out of wool they had donated for the cause.

Within three years the Skyelark flock had grown to the point that they needed to find other rangeland. This turned out to be easy. Local farmers were happy to have sheep mowing their orchards or clearing veggie stubble and adding nitrogen to the soil. Gillies and Alexis just had to set up and maintain the temporary electric fencing and water systems. It's hard to say who benefits more from these arrangements. "I know it could go either way with who pays whom,

depending on how long the sheep are there," says Gillies. "We've started out with handshake deals and a gift box of meat to the farmers. We did have an issue once where the sheep damaged some irrigation. We fixed it, but I think if we were going to offer mowing service to other than friends, a formal agreement would be a good idea."

Part of ranching is dealing with predators. Gillies and Alexis rely on their guardian dog who stays with the sheep. The dog replaces the top predator role whenever she is with the flock. But when the guard dog moves to another field the coyotes have their old place again. Gillies cautions, "If we were to displace the coyotes that are here, targeting them when they aren't causing problems, then new coyotes might move in and be more wise, or persistent. We can be part of a balance." So far the only two lambs they have lost were during the first year, before the dog was protecting them.

Chickens are another matter. "We had a bobcat coming around a lot and getting the poultry," acknowledges Alexis. "All we can really do is have electric fencing and close the coop at night." Luckily Skyelark Ranch is located in the middle of the valley, which doesn't have as much predator action as some other properties that border the back hills, or have the creek running through. They've proven that paying attention to wildlife corridors can make a big difference.

Both Gillies and Alexis are out working with the animals every day. Gillies does most of the website updates and social media, while Alexis handles direct correspondence on the phone, and writes the bills. "All the serious stuff," laughs Gillies.

Over time, their ideas for how the business would be run have changed. "Originally we thought we would do farmers' markets and a meat CSA," states Gillies, "but that has shifted over the years." They still sell at farmers' markets. They share a stand with Casa Rosa Farm and trade off weekends so their product can be at market without either farm attending every weekend. At farmers' markets people are often still amazed that there is fresh meat for sale, asking questions like, *How does this work? Do I have to sign up?*, to which Gillies and Alexis gladly respond, "No, you can get meat right here and now. You can bring home some bacon."

It was the CSA that fell by the wayside. They found they didn't have the time it takes to organize a CSA, and they didn't have a consistent or varied product. Through their first four years of selling meat, chicken was the one thing they could consistently offer on a monthly basis, not making for an interesting CSA to join. Their pork easily sells out at farmers' markets alone, and lamb is only available at certain times of year.

Ranching incomes often come in big chunks, with butchering happening somewhat seasonally. Eggs have provided the steady income that allowed Gillies to quit his other job. They collect anywhere from sixty to one hundred dozen eggs a day. The majority of these they sell through wholesale contracts. "It has been great to have wholesale outlets," says Alexis, "since if we have a slow day at market we can't freeze the eggs. We haven't taken the extra step and extra expense to get certified as organic, but the eggs are sold as pasture raised—which is better than just cage free."

Gillies and Alexis had not planned to sell in the wholesale market to butcher shops and restaurants. They seemed to have stumbled on this market by happy accident. They simply offered to sell Cornish Cross chickens to one butcher in the Bay Area and then through word of mouth were able to expand until they were selling to five butchers. This changed their focus to the wholesale market.

Since then they have stopped raising the Cornish hens. "The breed didn't fit with our overall model because every bird is coming in the mail from a giant conglomerate that has the genetic rights to that bird. Eight weeks later that bird is dead and we can't breed our own." They also found that with the shops needing fresh birds every week, the time managing birds and getting them to butchers was becoming overwhelming and other parts of the business were suffering. But at least they had made good connections with butchers who continue to want the meat they raise.

"We hope sheep will become the main focus of the ranch as the flock grows.

It's exciting for us to see the land management part of all this. We are fascinated to see what different animal rotations do to the soil. We've already seen a huge reduction in star thistle on the land. The sheep love it!"

KEEPING THE FARM

As much as forty percent of the nation's farmland may transfer hands in the next two decades, due to the rising age of farmers in America. There is also the problem of new farmers finding affordable land, as land prices near urban markets are often driven up based on what commuters, retirees and property investors can afford. Agricultural lease agreements, trusts and land succession plans can be ways to address these issues, but they can also be legally daunting. Fortunately there is assistance available in the form of many farmland conservation and protection programs nationwide.

California Farm Link is one such organization, which offers support in two main ways; a land access program and a farm opportunities loan program. The land access program offers a ongoing database of land for sale or lease and a complimentary database of farmers searching for land; meaning this service is available to both farmers and landowners. The loan program provides financing support for beginning, immigrant, or underserved farmers to obtain loans for equipment, infrastructure, or operating costs. Most of the people utilizing these services would otherwise have difficulty being approved for a loan, and farming requires substantial start-up funds not only in the beginning but every season thereafter. To date, California Farm Link has aided over 3,000 farmers in obtaining quality land and secure financing.

SPREADWING FARM

FARMING MODEL: PERMACULTURE FARMSTEAD

STARTED IN: 2010

OWNERS: CATHY SUEMATSU AND MICHAEL SMITH

SIZE: 5 ACRES

MAIN CROPS: FIGS, APRICOTS, PEACHES, PEPPERS, OKRA, AND GARLIC

Spreadwing Farm looks typical of many farms in their early years. There is the old farmhouse in need of major renovations, dirt paths winding through the weeds to the gardens, and laundry flapping in the wind. There is also the old barn, surrounded by goats and overflowing with stuff. Despite appearances, the barn is really well organized, and Cathy and Michael have done a lot of work to clean the place up from the previous owners.

As we sit around the kitchen table, next to stacked boxes of garlic, we discuss how any investment—of time or money—can be risky. Farming is obviously a time-honored risk, but no matter what choices we make, we have to wonder if they make sense. Does the cheaper housing price make it worth the commute? Are we saving enough to cover our retirement needs? I notice timelines, spreadsheets, and to-do lists posted on the wall. Michael and Cathy have wrestled with the big questions and come up with a unique plan.

They both knew that they didn't want to work a job just to pay the rent. Cathy came to the Capay Valley first, with her ex-partner Max. A friend introduced them

to the area and on their first visit Cathy, who studied entomology in college, saw a damselfly that she had never seen before. "I was fascinated by it," she recalls. After that visit they decided to rent a small house in Rumsey, and for a short time Cathy continued to commute for work as an entomologist. "A few years later, when I came to look at this property for sale I saw the damselfly again. We ended up buying this property. Those are the only two times in my life that I've seen that damselfly." It turned out to be a Spreadwing damselfly. "I wonder what will happen the next time I see one," Cathy says with a twinkle in her eye.

Not long after buying the property, Cathy and Max amicably parted ways. Before starting Spreadwing Farm, Cathy spent a few years working on local farms. She met Michael at a natural building workshop where he was teaching. Michael had been gardening for over fifteen years, for himself and communities he'd lived in. They are both interested in growing food and in having an intimate relationship with where their food comes from. But Michael explains, "Being a farmer is something I'm stepping into somewhat reluctantly—partly because I'm not much of a sales person and as a farmer that's part of the job: to sell food."

"I think there is little question that if we had jobs and we spent the same amount of time working as we do on our homesteading projects around here—growing and processing our own food—we would make more money," asserts Michael. "So from a purely economic standpoint it doesn't really make sense. But we don't want to do that; we want to be here with our kids every day, not running the rat race. We want to have that direct relationship with the food that we are putting into our bodies.

So that is why we are doing this. It's not about the money."

Cathy adds, "It's expensive to have a job. You have to pay for childcare, have a good car, get nice clothes." She estimates that at Spreadwing Farm they spend half their time doing homesteading activities that bring in little to no cash, and the other half of their time farming for commercial purposes. Hence the term farmsteading. They have a big vegetable garden and a herd of fourteen goats. From this they are able to supply most of their food needs for themselves, two

children, and an intern or two. They milk the goats and make cheese, and they dry, can, or ferment all kinds of veggies. Consequently, their grocery bill is very low. "We used to both drink a lot of black tea, but we are slowly weaning ourselves off things we can't produce ourselves. We still buy Cheddar cheese, but we probably sell more cheese than we buy."

Still, they do have a plan to make money. Max is still part owner of the property and they would like to eventually buy him out. Cathy and Michael have planted over 400 fruit trees. "Trees are what we see as being our long-term income." Meanwhile they have also been selling a lot of okra, as well as some peppers, garlic, and shallots. All of this farming is being done without a tractor. In 2014 they had their first year of surplus fruit to sell. They can foresee that taking care of their expanding orchard—harvesting, processing, and selling that fruit—will become a full-time job and a good income for several people.

They expect to go to one or two farmers' markets a week and continue to sell wholesale through outlets such as the Capay Valley Farm Shop. Obviously, fresh fruit doesn't hold very long so Cathy and Michael plan to sell dried fruit, jams, and other value-added products. "We are gaining a lot of experience now, with all the canning and fermenting we've been doing for ourselves," Cathy says with a smile. "In the future these homesteading skills should help us create some delicious goods."

They have also planned ahead by planting roughly sixty varieties of fruit trees. We take a walk, ducking through plastic deer fencing, and into the young orchard. This is a much more varied crop than most farmers plant, following more of a permaculture model. They planted many early and late varieties of peaches, apricots, and plums, as well as persimmons and figs. This was done to ensure that there would always be some fruit in season. "Some of these varieties may be less dependable," explains Michael, "but on the other hand, as the world's weather gets crazier, having all these varieties seems like a good insurance policy." As if on cue, the sun's rays break out of the clouds and warm our faces as we walk through the rows of thinly branched, six-foot-tall plum trees.

Spreadwing Farm may have already felt the effects of climate change on their farm. Many stone fruit varieties have a chill requirement, needing certain minimum hours of cold temperatures in order to have healthy flowering and good fruit. With a pensive frown Michael says, "Last year was mild and a lot of the stone fruit didn't taste right or it bruised earlier. Some locals attributed that to the lack of chill hours."

There were other mysterious problems with some of the fruit trees, such as peaches that ripened way ahead of time. Full Belly Farm had a similar problem, and they wondered if it might be from weather, or something else. Cathy and Michael talked with the University of California Cooperative Agriculture Extension office, which encouraged them to contact a laboratory. They had some leaves tested but nothing was glaringly wrong in those tests so they didn't get any answers.

Cathy has learned that problem solving is a big part of farming, and it's common to have more questions than answers. At Spreadwing Farm they have done plenty of experimenting. In one instance they were given bags of biochar, a charcoal soil amendment, with the agreement that they would run an experiment and share the data. Adding this amendment is a method to increase crop yields, familiar in permaculture circles. Cathy and Michael added the biochar to some holes as they planted the new orchard of bare-root fruit trees. They will analyze those trees, planted next to those without biochar, to see if the trees grow faster or produce more fruit. "I like problem solving," says Cathy. "We are still very much in a learning curve. And with fruit trees it's a much slower learning curve."

While they wait for the fruit trees to mature, Michael and Cathy do have a few other sources of income that help to slow the steady trickle out of their savings. Before farming, Michael had a busy career as a natural building instructor. He has co-authored several books about building with natural materials, from which he receives royalties. He still does occasional consulting, and teaches some workshops.

Spreadwing Farm would also not be possible without the help of interns. There are just too many things that need to happen every day. "We have a lot of experience combined between the two of us, so we find people who want to come and learn from us and that's a critical part of what makes this work," says Cathy. "It makes the relationship clear, too. The more people are clear about what they are coming here to learn, the better it works out."

Michael agrees. "Having interns is also a huge part of what helps us not feel isolated here. I've spent most of my life in a teaching mode and living in a community. It helps me feel like I'm doing something useful with my life, contributing to a bigger picture." The interns become an integral part of Speadwing Farm, helping in the garden and orchards, caring for the animals, preparing food in the kitchen, and taking turns with childcare. Michael and Cathy are also looking to share the property with like-minded business partners and to create community that way.

As they walk me to my car, I see a dragonfly buzzing over the trees. Maybe when the right partners show up, so will a third Spreadwing damselfly.

Photo credit Albert Straus

VIRIDITAS FARM

FARMING MODEL: ORGANIC PLANT BREEDING

STARTED IN: 1998

OWNER: SALLY FOX

SIZE: 130 ACRES

MAIN CROPS: COTTON, WHEAT, AND WOOL

'm not a real farmer," explains Sally Fox right off the bat. "I'm a plant breeder. I have been working since 1986 with the ancestor of this colored cotton." She holds up a fluffy boll of pinkish-brown cotton. Sitting on the couch, she is surrounded by baskets of cotton bolls, cotton yarn, and samples of cotton fabrics in shades of green or brown to off-white. The products of the farm are barely enough to fund the research Sally is doing. But Viriditas farm is a real farm, recently certified biodynamic. Sally produces organic, naturally colored Foxfiber® cotton, as well as heirloom Sonora wheat and Merino wool.

It takes a lot of time and money to develop a plant variety. Historically, before GMO seed companies took over, an independent plant breeder could receive royalties from seed companies that they could then use to fund more research. But when Sally Fox started her life's work there was not a market for organic, naturally colored cotton, there were no organic cotton farms, and there were no seed companies interested in paying her a royalty. Whenever she asked about growing cotton organically she perceived a lot of ridicule and negativity. "So unlike other breeders who could just send their seeds to real farmers for the trial crops, I had to do it all myself. And that's how it is that I became a farmer—very slowly and very clumsily," she says.

Sally found her destiny in a crumpled paper bag, while cleaning out a greenhouse. In college she had studied entomology, specializing in nematodes. She taught handspinning in college as a way to earn money, a hobby she had started when she was twelve years old. After finishing her master's degree in 1981, she found that there were hardly any jobs available. She was grateful to get a job with an independent plant breeder, Robert Dennett, who focused on tomatoes—and cotton. He was one of the first plant breeders to create hybrid tomatoes for the tomato processing industry. Sally was hired to grow vats of nematodes in order to test the resistance of Dennett's breeds.

It was only a part-time job, but Dennett said he would pay Sally for her time if she could make herself useful, so she started cleaning the greenhouse. There in a drawer she found a paper bag filled with bolls of brown cotton. Being a handspinner, Sally knew what she had found, and more than that, she saw a value there that hardly anyone at the time would have seen.

In one of her handspinning classes, she had met an older woman whose daughter had been a textile teacher in high schools, and this daughter had been dying fabrics without wearing gloves. The heavy metals in the dying process had migrated to her brain and she had been rendered a vegetable in a nursing home. Sally recalls, "When I learned that this woman's life was essentially ended by fabric dyes I became a complete fanatic about staying away from dyes and just using natural fibers. In college I made many things out of natural colored fibers. I even had an agreement with people at the SF Zoo, where they let me go collect musk ox and camel hair! In those days there weren't all these companies selling natural fibers. It wasn't a big hobby then; there were very few people spinning from raw fibers."

Sally had seen naturally colored cotton only once before, when someone from South America had brought it up to a hand weavers' convention in Santa Barbara. She was infatuated with it at the time, but then she didn't hear anything more about it until she opened that paper bag in Robert Dennett's greenhouse. She was excited to see this brown cotton, even though the fibers were short and coarse. She showed the bag to Dennett and demanded, "Where did this come from? Why aren't we breeding colored cotton?"

The story, as Dennett told Sally, was that the USDA breeder for California got the brown cotton from the Cajuns in Louisiana. "This was back in the days when there were USDA- and state-employed breeders, before GMOs took over the plant breeding industry," explains Sally. That brown cotton was known to be resistant to all disease, pests, and nematodes. So the idea was that this strain would be excellent germ plasma, to help make other varieties resistant. But Dennett had decided not to use it, reasoning that it was too hard to breed out the color, and that there was no market for colored cotton. Sally asked him, "Why don't we improve the fiber and make a market for colored cotton?"

"He was in his seventies and I was twenty-something," Sally remembers. "He started laughing and told me, *Why don't you improve the fiber and you create a market, in all this free time you have?* In other words, he wasn't going to pay me for this project."

So Sally got started. The first stage was the breeding and crossing and selecting, in much the same way as Gregor Mendel, "the father of modern genetics," did with peas. She went through the bag, picked out the seeds with the longest fibers, and planted them. That first brown cotton was a plant that grew in tropical climates; it was too big for machine picking and bloomed too late for temperate climates. She crossed those first plants with Pima S5, a cotton variety known for its long, strong fibers. She continued to cross various others, browns with browns and brown with Pima.

Cotton flowers usually only open for one day, and self-pollinate. The large flow-

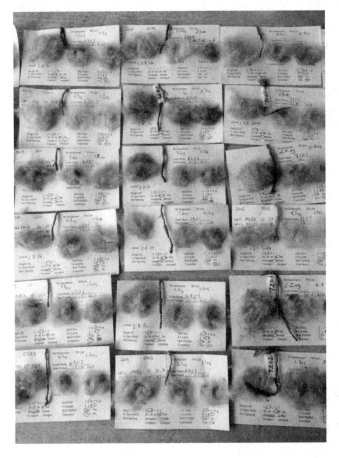

ers can be cut open one day early and the pollen pulled off. Sally says it's very easy and any normal tweezers will do it. Then the next day she brings the pollen to the flower she wants to cross it with. She tags that flower with the cross names. That's the first generation, F1. Later she takes the seeds from that plant and grows them to get an F2, and that's where individuality becomes apparent. From there, if the goal is to have an open pollinate variety, Sally can start to select for varieties. It takes an average of ten years from that first F1 cross to having a plant that is more or less genetically stable. It's taken almost thirty years for Sally to get to the stage where that plant is machine pickable, good for US climates, and has decent yield.

When finally Sally gets something that looks like a variety, then it can be sent to farms for trials. She and others have done a lot to promote an organic cotton market, so whereas thirty years ago there weren't any organic cotton farms, now there are. "I don't do the large-scale trials of varieties," says Sally, "so I don't call myself a real farmer."

She explains that a "real" farmer strives to give the plant the best of everything: good soil, no diseases or pests, no stress on the plants. In contrast, a breeder wants to grow plants that will be resilient and hardy. They want to see which seeds will survive hardships such as pests, depleted soils, or early frosts. "I choose plants that thrive in less than ideal conditions because you never know what the season is going to be like for the future farmer. So then when another farmer takes my seed and grows it in good conditions, it's hopefully going to really produce well."

In the year that Sally had her first F2s, she had about 1,500 plants of all the various crosses she had done. And among those plants was one scraggly plant that had two green cotton bolls. She crossed those seeds with some sea island cottons she'd gotten from the seed bank. "The green colored cotton was on a chromosome with a very weak fiber strength, but after a few generations there was a cross over event that allowed for the green color with strong and long fibers. I had roughly 800,000 plants growing, and I found that plant because I did the hard work of growing each generation, then looking at each plant, and feeling the fiber from each one —it was a one in a million chance! That was how I got my first Plant Variety Protection certificate (PVP). And that is the basis of all my work."

Each year since then, Sally has been making crosses and growing out new test plots. It's been a tough job for a woman. "In the beginning I had to get PVPs or no one would respect me. Other breeders treated me like I was silly and then later they insinuated that they could have done it faster or better."

Her first growing plots were near Bakersfield, California. That area has strict rules about cotton growing because historically it was a remote area and they wanted their cotton to be marketed together and to be of a certain quality—it's known as the Acala Cotton Quality District. Everyone had to grow the same variety. As a breeder, Sally had to be registered and the state had to come and inspect her nursery. By 1993, the Acala Cotton Quality District decided to outlaw colored cotton altogether, so Sally had to move. She went to Arizona and grew her test plots there until 1996, when again a quarantine on colored cotton was imposed. From there, she moved to Capay Valley. For a time things went well. She was selling her naturally colored cotton and continued to do more great work with the breeding. She fell in love and became a mother at age forty-one. Then after 2001 the US textile market went totally under.

"It was a very heartbreaking thing to watch," Sally recalls. The USA had been the largest textile manufacturer in the world, and suddenly that market was reduced by almost 90 percent. The textile mills were put out of business by mills in countries that dumped their dye wastes. The cost of cleaning dye waste can be double or triple the cost of the dying process, so countries with water regulations and cleanup systems have much higher costs. Other countries that may have had regulations but were not following them, undercut the market. All the big retailers went with them, abandoning the mills in the US, Europe, and Japan that had put millions of dollars into equipment to clean up the waste. "Most of my customers went out of business and the only one who didn't was the very first mill I had sold to—in Japan."

The Japanese mill provides yarn out of Sally's Foxfiber® cotton, but they haven't even been buying her colored cotton. They are buying an organic white cotton she bred. A large mill processes hundreds of bales at one time, and Sally only has about sixty acres for row crop farming, so it is farmers in New Mexico who grow a minimum of 100 acres of Sally's organic white cotton, and the mill pays her a commission to ship that cotton to Japan. "So that's another Ag job I do to support this breeding project," emphasizes Sally. "I handle orders and ship organic cotton grown by real farmers."

Since the US textile market crashed, Sally has been struggling to support her breeding work by selling the products from her farm. Her breeding work includes heirloom Sonora wheat, as well as sorghums and black-eyed peas. She is also breeding sheep and producing amazing merino wool fiber. She could write a book just on her experiences fending off coyotes. Most of the products of her farm are value added, needing to be shipped out for cleaning, spinning, etc. and then shipped back before selling. She does all this without any employees, and has little time to do marketing. "I'm just one person doing all this: the farm, the animals, and being a mom."

Sally says there is never a normal day on the farm. She plants in April and makes crosses in the summer. In autumn she has to walk all the rows of these test plots and look at each single plant to make the selections of which to save and plant the next year. Then she hand harvests her cotton and gins all these seeds with little research gins.

And everyday there are the animal chores. The money Sally earns from selling meat helps cover almost all the cost of having sheep. She raises them primarily for wool, doing select breeding to achieve a high fiber standard. The sheep are also important as a way to increase soil fertility. Viriditas Farm is Demeter certified as Biodynamic. This certification requires among other things that: at least ten percent of the farm's acreage be set aside for biodiversity, a majority of soil amendments be derived on-site from livestock and cover crops, and that fifty percent of the livestock's feed be grown on the farm. Sally tells me, "Going through the inspection and getting this certification was a lot of work!"

The drought has made Sally cautious. Growing cotton can take a lot of water. She says she could grow more cotton but doesn't want to run the risk of ruining her well and having to find money to drill a new one. Instead she is focusing on raising funds to purchase a scaled down gin that an engineer is designing for her. Sally says she would like to apply for grants but feels she is not in the loop with the right people. She has bales of colored cotton in storage that she could send to a mill in North Carolina, but first she has to get it ginned, and she can no longer risk sending it through a gin that has processed GMO cotton. That could ruin her seed supply.

Sally handles all her own sales. "My niche in all this is that I'm primarily the breeder and I'm also the grower of small quantities for people who want colored cotton—for handspinner customers and small designer clothing businesses. I'm just sticking with it and I've been sticking with it for a long time, through a lot of ups and downs." She sells yarn through her mail order business, and some bales of colored cotton to customers like the woman who buys about five bales a year to make high quality, Foxfiber® socks.

"I try to focus on what brings me pleasure—working with textile designers and with the plants themselves." Sally explains that she resonates with Michael Pollan's description in *The Botany of Desire*, where the plants attract humans in order to co-create new varieties. "I fall in love with the plants and I feel like I am their ambassador. That's what I enjoy—having this relationship with the plants where I'm not demanding that they produce. I'm not demanding anything, and that's what distinguishes me from a real farmer. A real farmer gives the plant everything the plant needs and asks that it produces for them as best as it can so that the farmers will be around for generations, to keep giving the plant what it needs. That is their agreement. My relationship with the plants is more like asking, *What do you want to be? What can you be? And what can I do to make a place for that in the world?* I've gotten to do this with two plants now, with the cotton and with wheat. And I'm beginning to fool around with milos (type of sorghums) and the black-eyed peas."

Sally is in her sixties now and believes that she has yet to master the craft of plant breeding. She tells the story of walking behind an older plant breeder in his eighties who came to look at her test plots. "He had this sense, and he would just walk through the rows and then stop right at the plant that was best for crossing. I have to meticulously look at each plant to identify that one, but he didn't need to do that; he could just tell." Sally is quiet for a moment and then continues, "I hope I can get to that point and I hope I keep coming up with ways to support my plant breeding. But I'm grateful that I have gotten to this point at least."

PATENTS AND PVPS
OR PROTECTING INTELLECTUAL PROPERTY

Plant breeding for a stable new variety can be expensive and require a commitment of seven to ten years. In order to ensure that plant breeders can continue their work, they need protection and a way to recover their investment in experimentation.

Plant patenting has received some bad press, with stories of farmers who have been sued for growing plants, and people opposed to genetic modification of food in general. But there are three ways for plant breeders to protect their intellectual property.

In the United States, Plant Patents and Utility Patents are available through the U.S. Patent and Trademark Office. Utility Patents apply to sexually reproduced plants whereas Plant Patents apply to asexually reproduced plants. Plant Variety Protection (PVP) certificates are granted by the USDA Plant Variety Protection Office, and apply to sexually reproduced plants and tubers. PVP Certificates are much less expensive than Patents and they provide less protection for the breeder. The three types of protections last for sixteen to twenty years.

The PVP act of 1970 allows two exemptions to the owner's exclusive control of a variety. These are the researcher's and the farmer's exemption. The researcher's exemption allows others to conduct research with the variety, including using the protected variety in crosses to create a new variety. The farmer's exemption allows farmers to save seeds from a PVP variety and replant those seeds without breaking the law. The farmer can't sell those seeds, but he doesn't have to pay the seed company again to replant them, as is the case with patented varieties.

The Utility Patent holder can exclude others from propagating, growing, using, or selling the protected material without permission, and there is no researcher's or farmers' exemption. So protected material cannot be used without permission in a breeding program or be saved for personal use by farmers.

Sources: http://articles.extension.org/pages/18449/intellectual-property-protection:-what-do-i-need-to-know-when-growing-and-breeding-organic-crops- and http://perennialpatents.com/plantpatent-v-utility-patents/

PLANT BREEDERS HISTORY

It's been just over twenty years since Monsanto first patented its GMO corn. Since then the careers of plant breeders have changed dramatically. There are almost no independent breeders making a living off their work anymore. Meanwhile, government and university plant breeding positions are now often funded heavily by genetic engineering companies.

Before genetic engineering took over, there were plenty of independent plant breeders. There also used to be many more USDA- and state-employed breeders growing their test plots on university or public lands, all paid for by taxpayers. Since the 1970s, when a breeder developed a variety they applied for a PVP and then licensed their varieties to seed companies, receiving royalties for the sale of the seeds. But in Sally's experience, nowadays big seed companies are only interested in licensing a breeder's varieties if they are patented. And patents, being expensive, are generally used for genetically engineered crops.

In 1994, a survey was conducted to determine the number of science person years (SY) that were devoted to plant breeding research and development in the United States public and private sectors. The study authors found that over the five-year period of 1990–1994, the net loss of plant breeding SYs in State Agricultural Experimental Stations (SAES) was estimated to be 12.5, or 2.5 SYs per year. For the same period, private industry was estimated to have grown by 160 SYs. A follow-up survey in 2001 found 108 fewer plant breeders employed by the SAES, a 21 percent decline since the 1994 survey.

It's also interesting to note that in 2013, there were 1,099 plant patent applications granted by the US Patent and Trademark office. Corporations own 855 of these, while only 235 are owned by private individuals, and 9 are owned by the US Government.

"Even in the organic seed market, where people say they want organic varieties, most of the time they don't want to provide any kind of protection for the breeder. Is everyone independently wealthy except me?!" laments Sally Fox. She doesn't even bother applying for PVPs anymore because it takes time and money, and she hasn't been able to license the four PVPs she has.

Breeders used to sell their license to companies who would grow and sell the seeds. But that system got dismantled by the genetic engineering companies when they bought up the seed companies. "I don't know if in this country we will ever recover from this take over," Sally says. "But unless there is massive funding from the public, there is no way for the independent plant breeder to do all this work and then give away all the seeds. That's the thing that doesn't compute."

Sources

https://nifa.usda.gov/sites/default/files/resource/Public%20Sector%20Plant%20Breeding%20Resources%20in%20the%20U.S..pdf

https://nifa.usda.gov/sites/default/files/resource/National%20Plant%20Breeding%20Study-1.pdf

http://www.uspto.gov/web/offices/ac/ido/oeip/taf/plant.pdf

WEST VALLEY FARMS

FARMING MODEL: AGRIBUSINESS

STARTED IN: 1999

OWNERS: THE HATANAKA FAMILY

SIZE: 6,000 ACRES

MAIN CROPS: TOMATOES AND ALMONDS

Driving from the town of Capay, past Esparto and toward Woodland, it's a familiar sight to see acres and acres of commercially farmed tomatoes and long rows of almond trees. Some of these are part of West Valley Farms, owned by the Hatanaka Family. Jason Hatanaka, dressed in jeans and work boots, meets me at the farm office in a modest office rental building on the west end of Woodland. Inside there is a large, sparse room where two employees are quietly working at their desks. Photos of almond blossoms hang on the wall, and I notice a few Ziploc bags filled with samples of shelled and unshelled almonds on the counter. Jason invites me into the conference room next door, where we sit in comfy chairs at the head of a large oval table.

The Hatanaka family has been farming in and around Capay Valley for three generations. Today, they farm about 6000 acres, with almonds as their main crop. They started planting almonds in 1998. That turned out to be the perfect time to plant, just ahead of the big almond boom. They now have trees ranging from one to eighteen years old.

Jason's grandfather, John Hatanaka, came home to Capay after WWII and started farming around the Esparto area. (During the war he had been held in a detention camp and then released to fight in an infantry battalion, but that's another story.) He grew tomatoes and all kinds of vegetable row crops. "My grandfather, who is still alive today at ninety-two years old, bought one of the first mechanical tomato harvesters," Jason recalls. "He also developed his own mechanical nut harvester—might have been one of the first ones built, but he never patented it. I remember seeing it when I was young; it was very similar to the machines they use today. He was very innovative for his time."

Jason's father later took over and expanded the farm. Terry Hatanaka started with about five hundred acres of crops, and that progressed into about six thousand acres of tomatoes, most of that land being leased. "It was my dad's theory," says Jason, "that in growing row crops you have more profit margin if you are leasing land, since the cost of buying land is so much higher than an agricultural lease. And he was right." Then Jason tilts his head to one side and throws a hand up. "I mean, if we had purchased land way back when, it would have been beneficial when the land prices went through the roof, but we weren't in the real estate business; we're farmers." The Hatanakas became specialists in the tomato crop.

"Growing up, I used to go to work with my dad," Jason shares. "He would drop me off at the shop and I would hang out with the guys, or I'd play in the dirt, where I had my own little farm with my toy tractors. I have a brother and sister, but I guess I was the one who enjoyed the stink of the tomatoes, so I'm the one who carried on the family business." His father, now in his sixties, is still involved in the family business, helping with a lot of the business decisions.

In Jason's time at West Valley Farms, he's seen a lot of change. They've always grown tomatoes, but have also done sunflowers, rice, wheat, and even sugar beets. At various times they have planted as far north as Artois, and as far south as Dixon. In the tomato days they were growing in three counties. That meant covering a lot of ground. Jason used to commonly put seventy-five thousand miles a year on his vehicle. "I spent a lot of time sleeping under overpasses. It was pretty intense. I used to do double shifts, just go home for four hours between 2 a.m. and 5 p.m. I liked that intensity, such as fixing the tomato harvester quick so we could get the harvest done on time. It was an adrenalin rush. But I was twenty years younger so I had the energy."

Jason is now the vice president of the corporation, acting as a general manager, overseeing operations. "The last ten years I've migrated into this office, which is okay. It's a lot more stressful here than it is out there. We have grown." West Valley Farms has about sixty employees, and additionally they hire outside labor contractors for pruning and other tasks. "I oversee it all," says Jason. "But we have a lot of specialists. One guy that specializes in irrigation, another who specializes in tractor work, and there is the shop work manager—everyone has his or her own responsibility. At our farm we have always had the motto 'No Bosses.' Everyone here works together to accomplish the same goals. So that's why we have people like Juan, who's sixty-three and started working for us under my grandfather when he was seventeen. So he's been here the whole time and is now like a family member. We have multiple employees who've been with us over twenty years."

Today, West Valley is still farming about six thousand acres, but they have put in more permanent crops and the dollars have changed. They own about six hundred acres, much of that purchased recently for the almonds, and they plan to acquire more land. But they still see leasing as a fine way to go. "We've got some good leasing relationships. Much of the land we lease for almonds is owned by old families that acquired it through homesteading long ago, and some of our row crop land is owned by large corporations, like the gravel mine."

In addition to the almonds and tomatoes, they still do crop rotations, resting the ground and replenishing the soil. "We try to make some money off the crop rotation," explains Jason. "Corn stalks add organic material to the ground that is good for the tomatoes, but it's not a good cash crop. And corn takes a lot of water. Ten years ago I could make an okay amount of money on corn, but I haven't grown it recently. Of course the money is in the tomatoes and almonds, and we've got the best climate for them."

Northern California almonds don't actually perform as well on average as Southern California, as far as yields per acre. Southern California almond growers expect 3,000 pounds per acre, minimum. West Valley has seen yields of 4,000 pounds an acre in a rare year. But their average range from their various orchards is from 1,500 pounds to over 3,500 pounds. "We don't have the same soil or climate conditions as Southern California, but at least we have water," says Jason emphatically.

Despite feeling secure about the local water sources, Jason is conservative with water use. He knows almonds have gotten negative press as a thirsty crop. "We bury our drip irrigation, which I say is like an IV for the plant. We do that for tomatoes and for almonds. It's expensive, like $1,200 an acre just for the irrigation system!" He says he's had drip tape that has lasted five years, as long as there aren't rodent problems. "Mice need to chew just to keep their teeth growing so they just go along the tape and gnaw away. We see the water puddle up on top and then we have to go replace sections. The guys have gotten creative with how to re-thread the channel while pulling out the ruined piece. If it's only a few feet long that works."

West Valley Farms have mostly Nonpareil almonds. They also grow at least eight other varieties. "We want different types to account for early and late varieties and the need for different pollinators. We have to come back and harvest on different days and that can complicate things. Some varieties come forty-eight days after the Nonpareil, but those types have a hard shell so they can get rained on and it's no big deal."

Nonpareils are soft shell almonds and if it rains on them near harvest, the water penetrates to the nut and can ruin the crop. "It gets exciting sometimes, but

Transplanting tomatoes. Photo credit Patrick Garrison

nothing like a tomato crop," exclaims Jason. "When you get rain on a tomato you have less than six days to get it off the field before it goes bad."

West Valley Farms do not have their own processing facility to take the nuts down to the meat form. They harvest and then take the almonds to a huller-sheller plant. Sometimes that sheller is also the handler they sell to, but more often now they just hold the crop in the shells and then move the almonds from there to a handler. "Whereas we used to be in a pool with other growers, delivering nuts and then walking away and waiting until they sent us a check, now we call our own sales. We deliver and then we follow the market ourselves and then we say when to sell this many containers."

Jason gets emails with updates on where the price of almonds should fall, or where it stands on a daily basis. They do their own marketing, making a phone call and selling to a handler, who sells to a broker, who then sells to the end user. "So yep, it touches hands several times and everybody gets a fee per pound, and we are still basically at the bottom."

Jason acknowledges that they could cut out the middleman. Companies in India and South Korea who want to buy directly have recently contacted him. "It's interesting, but we have yet to do it. It would require another whole area of expertise for our business, and we'd probably have to buy and operate our own huller-sheller. We'd rather grow the crops and let other people deal with all that."

I ask Jason if nut crops are easier than row crops, and he laughs. "Orchardists are often portrayed as the lazy farmers. Orchards may be less intense than perishable crops because you have a little elbowroom on when to act, but it's still a constant workflow. I think we are successful because we have taken the intensity of what we learned growing tomatoes and applied it to the orchards." Jason continues, "I particularly like the orchards better because when you go out into the fields you walk in the shade. Also I enjoy eating almonds whereas I never liked tomatoes. I tried but never acquired a taste for raw tomatoes."

From Jason's perspective the almond boom has been great, and the tomato industry has been nothing but headache. His father sees the tomato days as the good old days. "He and his friends get together and tell stories about all the crazy fun times they had, and the expensive wine they used to drink. They were making unbelievable money."

I was surprised to learn from Jason that the tomato industry used to have a reputation as a corrupt industry. Some growers would bribe the field man from the cannery to give them the best contracts. But the Hatanaka family looked down on that kind of corruption.

The payment schedule for commodity tomatoes is based on the cannery schedule. Before planting, the farmer gets a contract and delivery schedule with the cannery, to deliver a certain amount of tomatoes on a certain week. In that way, the farmer knows how much to plant. The cannery has to coordinate with all the farmers to keep the cannery running at full capacity, or at least 80 percent of capacity. If all the local tomatoes came ripe at the same time, the cannery would be overloaded and the fruit would rot. If there was a gap in ripening times then the cannery would have to shut down, which is a huge cost because every time they start back up they have to re-clean the facility and check for sterility. West Valley works with only two canneries now, whereas they used to work with six or eight. Some canneries have moved to Mexico, but there are still canneries nearby in Woodland, Williams, and Dixon.

For the farmer to stay on schedule, they have to consider the different varieties of tomatoes and plant them at different times to have the harvest at the right time. "All the scheduling is done on spreadsheets now," Jason assures me. "The cannery tells us how many tons of which variety they need, by what date. So I put that information into my spreadsheet and it tells me what date range to plant, with a two- or three-day window. The season usually takes care of itself though. Like this year we were two weeks behind schedule getting planted, because of the spring rains, and now we have already caught up because of these last two weeks of high heat."

"Corporate farming is somewhat boring compared to smaller family farms," reflects Jason. "I mean, everything is so systematic. We use every type of technology we can get our hands on. We have moisture sensors in the ground, it's all tied in to a computer, Internet based. We have weather stations in the orchards to look at temperatures, wind. Tractors steer themselves nowadays; there are operators inside but they steer automatically. Eventually they will run without an operator inside. Just like in the automotive industry where everything has gone to robotics. Then again, labor laws this day and age make it hard as an employer. The ability to work hard seems to be gone in this new generation."

"But Mother Nature has a strange way of doing things," he admits. "About the time you think you are going to have the best year ever, she comes in and wipes it.

I follow weather patterns to see if there is any pattern from past years. It's a crap-shoot, but we get it right sometimes. You do everything you can do as a farmer to give yourself the best chance. I enjoy the challenge. I like to see progress. I like to groom the fields, preparing the transplants for the next level. I also like to compete with my father's high yield records, but it's not really fair to him because he's not farming today, and it's different every year."

"It's kind of like what they told me as a kid playing baseball: you have to leave it all on the field. As long as you give it your all, then even if you don't win, at least you know you gave it your all. Same thing in farming; I leave it all on the field."

UPDATES

Since the time of these interviews, there have been a few changes worth mentioning. Annie Hehner has married a fellow farmer and they are now raising daughter Ada along with veggies, fruits and chickens. And Spreadwing Farm has taken on another family as business partners, though there have been no further sightings of the spreadwing damselfly.

Photo credit Fran Lewis

ACKNOWLEDGEMENTS

I want to thank my son Sha'an first and foremost, as he has had to share my attention with this book more than anyone else. And I am gratefully in debt to his father Todd, who sustains me with delicious homegrown food while I am preoccupied with writing.

When the idea of this book first came to me, it was Paul Muller and Dru Rivers who helped me expand my vision to a diversity of farms. And it would not have been written without Brinkley Hutchins, who was this book's midwife. Her coaching helped me take the idea from conception, to manuscript in small, joyful steps.

I also wish to thank Keli Rutan-Jorgensen for transcribing and early editing, Aaron Sikes for his editing and confidence boosting, Michael Smith for the moral support, Christiana Paoletti, Frances Blaine, and Paula Kelsall for sharing insights, Anna Brait for her mark-ups, and all the Capay Valley people who have given me their time for interviews and photos.

This book would not have been the same without the innovative freelancers at Reedsy.com. From helping to choose a title, to final proofreading, they were my publishing team. A big thanks goes to Ashley Halsey, who gracefully dealt with my inexperience as she worked to create the beautiful cover and interior designs.

CPSIA information can be obtained
at www.ICGtesting.com
Printed in the USA
FSOW04n1645200917
38990FS